Praise from leaders in early childhood education

"Through this reflective work and its myriad examples including illustrative photographs, resources, and planning tools, Eric Nelson unveils the essential elements for establishing and supporting highly engaging quality outdoor environments for young children. This book provides a developmental framework that early childhood practitioners, administrators, and trainers need to effectively address this extremely important aspect of children's play and learning."

> —Ed Greene, PhD, Senior Advisor of Piramide Approach to Early Learning, Cito USA/ Netherlands and Facilitator at JCCEO Head Start Center of Excellence in Birmingham

"The outdoor classroom is a healthy, engaging, and creative response to today's educational challenges. *Cultivating Outdoor Classrooms* provides the why and how in an accessible format that any educational leader can use to transform the learning environment at their school site. Photographs, design plans, a defined process of staff engagement, as well as curricular ideas and the information you need to begin this transformation, are all here. Educators would do well to embrace these concepts."

> —Renatta M. Cooper, Coauthor of *Playing to Get Smart* and President of the Pasadena Unified School District Board of Education

"With *Cultivating Outdoor Classrooms*, there are no more excuses for the same-old, same-old behaviors and routines in early childhood programs. Now, everyone can learn how to build a practical, useful, and exciting outdoor classroom at any site. Preschool children today do not spend nearly enough quality time playing outdoors—not at home, and not in school. Denying children ample outdoor playtime has developmental and academic consequences. *Cultivating Outdoor Classrooms* highlights these risks, and gives solid evidence for the value of time spent outside playing. Eric's enthusiasm for the outdoors and for giving children the opportunity to learn in nature is translated into a text that is meaningful for everyone who works with young children. Pages of wonderful photographs help to inspire ideas and give concrete examples for easy steps teachers can take *today* toward changing spaces and making outdoor learning accessible for children in school programs. *Cultivating Outdoor Classrooms* is both a foundational how-to book for educators taking their first steps toward the joy of working with children outdoors, and, for more experienced educators, a confirmation of their best practices. This book inspires me to continue working with teachers, parents, and other school directors as they explore the possibilities of creating outdoor classrooms at their school sites!"

> —Sheryl E. Cohen, PhD, Director of Stephen S. Wise Temple Early Childhood Center, President of BJE-Early Childhood Director's Network, and Vice President Programming of the National Jewish Early Childhood Network

"Eric Nelson understands the profound benefits children gain from daily access to natural outdoor classrooms. His comprehensive and thoughtful book outlines practical strategies for making this wonder-filled learning a way of life in early childhood programs. *Cultivating Outdoor Classrooms* will support and inspire teachers and administrators as they begin an exciting journey toward a fulfilling new way of working with children. Research continues to show the adverse effects of children's disconnection from nature and the positive gains possible when daily nature connections are supported by caring, engaged adults. The ideas in this book are needed today more than ever."

—Nancy Rosenow, Coauthor of *Learning with Nature Idea Book* and Executive Director of Dimensions Educational Research Foundation/Nature Explore

"Eric Nelson has created the definitive textbook for training new early childhood educators about the importance of bringing nature into the lives of children and helping them to become independent learners. He provides practical steps teachers can take to become agents of change in their schools. From beginning discussions, to planning, to implementation, *Cultivating Outdoor Classrooms* gives wonderful examples of what teachers can do in their current environments to engage children in the wonder of learning."

—Shelley Gonzales, MA, Adjunct Faculty and Child Development Center Laboratory School Director at West Valley College in Saratoga, CA

Cultivating Outdoor Classrooms

Cultivating Outdoor Classrooms

Designing and Implementing Child-Centered Learning Environments

ERIC NELSON

Redleaf Press®
www.redleafpress.org
800-423-8309

Published by Redleaf Press
10 Yorkton Court
St. Paul, MN 55117
www.redleafpress.org

Excerpt on pages 126–127 from the Preschool Outdoor Environment Measurement Scale (POEMS) website by Karen DeBord, Linda Hestenes, Robin Moore, Nilda Cosco, and Janet McGinnis. Reprinted by permission of the POEMS Development Team.

First edition 2012
Cover design by Jim Handrigan
Cover photograph © Edmund Barr. Reprinted by permission.
Interior design by Erin Kirk New
Typeset in Adobe Chapparal Pro
Printed in the United States of America
22   21   20   19   18   17   16   15   3   4   5   6   7   8   9   10

Library of Congress Cataloging-in-Publication Data
Nelson, Eric M .
    Cultivating outdoor classrooms : designing and implementing child-centered learning environments / Eric Nelson.
        p. cm.
    Summary: "There are many ways outdoor spaces can be transformed into fully functioning classrooms where children explore, experiment, and spend quality time in nature. Filled with both simple and large-scale ideas, Cultivating Outdoor Classrooms provides support as you design and implement outdoor learning environments."
    —Provided by publisher.
    Includes bibliographical references.
    ISBN 978-1-60554-025-2 (pbk.)
    1. Outdoor education. 2. Outdoor education—Study and teaching. 3. Experiential learning.   I. Title.
    LB1047.N39 2012
    371.3'84—dc23
                                        2011045602

Printed on acid-free paper

To my granddaughter, Haley Ella Hom, and all those of her generation, that their world be a better place.

Contents

Foreword

How did you play as a child? Where did you play? What did you learn by playing?

Probably (depending on how old you are) you got to play outdoors, investigating a complex and often unpredictable world of nature and negotiating relationships with friends. As many adults will remember, but many children today have never discovered, the richest learning environments are outdoors. In contrast, many children today spend all their time indoors, in activities programmed by adults to teach right answers to children.

It's February in Los Angeles, where I live. The sun is shining, the grass is green, and there's snow on the mountains. The birds are busy and noisy, but where are the four-year-olds? They're sitting at the tables indoors, getting wigglier every minute. Real learning happens outdoors too. It's time to go out—and *move*.

I learned to teach young children at the University of Wisconsin–Madison, where February is quite a different experience. But we took our little badgers outdoors every day, where they used all their large muscles and explored snow and ice and frosty breath, and we either stood and shivered or sensibly joined them and ran around too. Children, as I learned then and have been confirming ever since, are active learners—acquiring physical knowledge and social-emotional knowledge and co-constructing cognitive knowledge not only by sitting and listening, but especially by doing. And there's more to do outdoors—more space, more sensory materials, more unpredictability, more open-ended tasks in which the outcomes haven't been predetermined by adult planners. "If I do this, what will happen?" the three-year-old thinks, and then she does it, and finds out.

Prehistorically, much of human intelligence was developed in response to the challenges posed by the natural world: what can we do when we find ourselves cold, wet, sunburned, thirsty, hungry, or being snarled at? Children deprived of all such challenges simply won't be as smart as those as those with opportunities to confront nature for themselves, temporarily separated from heating, air-conditioning, and nonstop video.

"The teacher's contribution to play always begins with the physical environment, with stage setting. Developmentally, physical knowledge comes first. . . . It's up to adults to provide enough space, enough materials, and enough time, by arranging the environment so the play can happen" (Jones and Reynolds 2011, 21).

And almost anything that can be done indoors can also be done outdoors. What activities can we take outside? What will the children learn from them?

I've known Eric Nelson for many years through our shared experience at Pacific Oaks College and Children's School, and in 2003 when his Child Educational Center received funding from Los Angeles County for a five-year project "to increase the quantity, quality, and benefit of outdoor experiences for children ages 0 to 5 in Los Angeles County child care centers," I jumped at the chance to join its educational team. We offered teachers weekend opportunities to play in an Outdoor Classroom themselves, share their experience, and reflect on what they could do in their own settings. We learned too. What's an Outdoor Classroom? How can you create one? How can you convince others that it's where young children learn best?

In this outstanding guide for teachers, decision makers, and parents, Eric Nelson offers solidly documented background on why and how to overcome nature deprivation in children's daily experience in preschool.

Elizabeth Jones, PhD
Faculty Emerita, Pacific Oaks College

Jones, Elizabeth, and Gretchen Reynolds. 2011. *The Play's the Thing: Teachers' Roles in Children's Play*. 2nd ed. New York: Teachers College Press.

Acknowledgments

THIS BOOK evolved from thirty-five years of experience with ECE environments, programs, professionals, and others associated with early care and education. None of that would have mattered had David Heath of Redleaf Press not approached me after a presentation with the invitation to write it. I am most indebted and grateful to the contribution the entire Redleaf team has made in bringing the work to publication.

My professional path, not to mention the subject matter of the book, was the combined result of the contributions of many individuals and organizations. My parents, Stanley and Dorothy Nelson, provided me with a childhood that allowed me to experience the outdoors on my own, starting as a very young child, establishing a personal reference point for all that I do. Sally Smith Graney initially opened the door to the world of working with young children, and Betsy Hiteshew started me on my professional path and mentored me along the way. My educational experience as a graduate student at Pacific Oaks College under the tutelage of Molly Scudder and the PO faculty during the 1970s provided me the theoretical and practical foundation for my Outdoor Classroom work.

More recently Betty Jones, Sharon Stine, and Renatta Cooper all contributed to my first efforts at articulation and sharing of Outdoor Classroom philosophy and practices. Important psychological and philosophical concepts are drawn from my graduate study at the University of Santa Monica under the leadership of Drs. Ron and Mary Hulnick. A special thanks is owed to Richard Louv, whose *Last Child in the Woods* has ignited a renewal of the return-to-nature movement for children and families and helped me cultivate important elements of my thinking about the need for the Outdoor Classroom.

Experience from activities in the field has been fundamental to articulating the Outdoor Classroom concept and practice. For over thirty years the development of the model Outdoor Classroom has flourished at my place of work, the Child Educational Center, Caltech/JPL Community (CEC), through the participation and support of children, parents, staff, and boards of trustees, as well as the California Institute of Technology and the Jet Propulsion Laboratory. CEC program director Lisa Cain-Chang and a host of CEC long-tenured teachers have nurtured that model, establishing a guiding set of practices and substantial body of fieldwork.

My early consulting with Dennis Hudson helped me to articulate design concepts, as have design partnerships with Ronnie Sigel. ALA funding from First 5 LA enabled me to first articulate the Outdoor Classroom idea. Continuing funding from the Orfalea Foundations, with the guidance and support of Adrianna Foss and Lois Mitchell, has enabled me to further develop Outdoor Classroom concepts while working in depth with most of the child care centers in Santa Barbara County. Teachers, directors, and parents from hundreds of centers have been both generous and gracious in sharing their experience of implementing their Outdoor Classrooms.

As that implementation has spread, the members of the Outdoor Classroom Demonstration Site executive committee have been constant contributors of ideas and a source of support along with my Los Angeles administrator and friend of over twenty-five years, Lynn Farwell. Ellen Veselack, CEC preschool director and my frequent co-presenter, and Theresa Embry, my Santa Barbara work partner, have been instrumental in cultivating hundreds of Outdoor Classrooms while providing me with a steady source of stories and learning from the field.

Last, but foremost, I would not have been able to write the book without the steadfast love, infinite patience, encouragement, and contributions of my wife and work partner of over thirty years, Elyssa Nelson, CEC executive director. Our lifetime collaboration has made it all possible.

Cultivating Outdoor Classrooms

The Role of the Outdoor Classroom

THE OUTDOOR CLASSROOM is a philosophy and a practice that benefits all children, particularly those enrolled in early childhood education (ECE) programs. In this book, you will learn how to create the Outdoor Classroom, guided by these premises:

1. Education is not an end in itself. Early childhood education is much more than preparing children for K–12 programs; its first and foremost responsibility is to honor the process of childhood and the uniqueness of each individual child as it supports every child in realizing his or her full potential.

2. Effective programs for children reflect a vision and a set of values. The Outdoor Classroom is built on the premise that society seeks to serve the highest good.

3. Process is as important as content in the Outdoor Classroom: children learn as much from their teachers, the environment, and the program's vision as from the content of a curriculum.

Note on Implementing the Outdoor Classroom in Challenging Climates
The Outdoor Classroom Project, from which the content of this book evolved, began in Southern California. Many of the examples in this book are taken from that location. The philosophy, principles, and practices are, however, applicable in all climates. This is discussed in more detail in chapter 2.

Looking Back at the 1950s

There is something to be said for the view that the quality of childhood peaked in the United States in the 1950s. Two world wars and the Great Depression were over. The economy was strong. One of the great scourges of twentieth-century childhood, polio, was on its way to defeat. Many families could afford for the mother to stay at home. Pressures on most children were low: school demands were mild, summer was still downtime, and children probably had more time on their own than at any other point in American history.

Clearly, not all children had golden childhoods in the 1950s. But some elements of that era provide useful reference points when we look at what is happening to childhood today:

- Children spent much of their time outside, often in natural settings.

- Children enjoyed a lot of unstructured free time.

- Children spent much of their time with little or no adult supervision.

Compare these conditions to those of most children today, and you can see what a difference fifty years has made. Today far fewer children enjoy unstructured outdoor play. Instead, the majority of American children have become preoccupied with electronic devices. Physical inactivity, along with changes in diet, have produced an epidemic of obesity among children. Diagnoses of attention deficit disorder steadily increase. More and more children lack any meaningful contact with nature.

How the Outdoor Classroom Can Address These Problems

The Outdoor Classroom addresses the problems facing children today with certain principles, elements, characteristics, and tenets:

Principles

- Time—Children benefit from spending substantial time outdoors.

- Activities—Even with a minimally developed yard, there are very few children's activities that cannot be done outside.

- Initiation—Children's development is optimized when they spend a significant amount of time participating in child-initiated activities that are teacher supported.

- Nature—Children need a connection to nature in order to be whole.

Key Elements

- Teachers and program directors must *be interested* in the Outdoor Classroom and *committed* to making it happen.

- Teachers and program administrators must have the *skills and knowledge* to make it happen.

- *Physical resources* are needed to support the Outdoor Classroom (toys, equipment, etc.).

- Parents, executive management, and owners or governing boards of centers must *allow*, and hopefully *support*, the Outdoor Classroom.

Characteristics

- Children spend substantial *periods of time* outside, and it is easy and safe for them to get there; they are free to move easily between the indoors and outdoors.

- *Space* is available for all activities, including running.

- A full range of activities are available for children to participate in, including many activities that are traditionally thought of as "indoor activities," even when there isn't a fully developed yard.

- While outside, children frequently initiate their own activities.
- Children are engaged with their activities, and the teachers are actively engaged with them.
- The outdoor program supports continuous learning and the fact that children are learning all the time.
- The outdoor curriculum is a distinct and robust part of the overall program and changes with children's changing needs and interests.

Tenets

- Learning occurs everywhere and all the time.
- Outdoors, the process of mastering the fundamentals of literacy, math, and science is greatly enhanced in a curriculum that is holistic and complete.
- The foundation of cognitive development and success in later life begins with, and relies on, physical activity during the critical first five years of brain development.

To implement the Outdoor Classroom successfully, you'll need the following:

- a vision of what you want to achieve
- an awareness of the challenges facing today's children
- a grasp of developmental theory
- an understanding of the Outdoor Classroom's principles and practices
- the ability to assess children's progress in the Outdoor Classroom

Preschool Politics and Play

For decades, the role of play in children's development has been a contentious issue. Advocates for adult-driven academic programs have quarreled with advocates for children's right to unstructured, self-initiated play. Recent funding emphasis on kindergarten readiness as well as the standards movement have intensified the stakes in this battle. Advocates for the importance of play have responded by forming groups like the International Play Association, the American Association for the Child's Right to Play, and the National Institute for Play. Recent books pleading the case of play include Elizabeth Jones and Renatta M. Cooper's *Playing to Get Smart* and David Elkind's *The Power of Play*.

The efforts of advocates for play are grounded in the belief that children learn best through play—that like other mammals, children develop physically, cognitively, psychologically, emotionally, socially, and linguistically through play. Children are hardwired for play; it's how they learn about themselves, other people, and the world around them.

If learning through play is completely natural to children, where does adult-designed learning fit in? The Outdoor Classroom's answer is it must fit in *very carefully,* particularly for very young children. Adult-designed programs are commonly accompanied by adult expectations and standards (and these, in turn, characterize some efforts by children as "mistakes"). Everyone learns best when relaxed. Play, almost by definition, is relaxing and open ended.

During unstructured play, children only need to satisfy themselves. They can try something over and over until it satisfies them and their companions. They are not forced to compete with each other or be evaluated by adult standards. They participate when and how they feel comfortable. Their play is usually seamless, moving from one plot or interest to another. Play reflects the natural rhythms of children's concentration and curiosity. When opportunities for play occur in enriched environments, children develop the skills that formal education strives for: literacy, math, and science.

Unstructured play is imperiled today. What passes for play in many ECE programs is more a product of adult and commercial influences than it was fifty years ago. Nonetheless, adults who are devoted to child-centered play can protect and nurture play that is structured naturally by children's initiative rather than by adults.

Between the social factors that discourage children's play and the emphasis on adult-defined outcomes in ECE programs, it is amazing that play can hold its own anymore as a valued linchpin in children's lives. The Outdoor Classroom turns play into an adult-supported child-led learning strategy in ECE programs.

A New Guiding Vision for Early Childhood Education

Childhood is a critical stage of human growth. While I watched my daughter nursing and caring for her new child recently, I marveled at how a nine-month gestation had produced a healthy baby. I realized how much more work and focus would be needed to guide that child forward into a mature and healthy adulthood. As difficult as pregnancy was for my daughter, she now faces a much longer and more complex task, as do her husband and all of the people who will be part of her daughter's young life.

Children need a nurturing childhood to emerge as healthy, whole adults, just as fetuses need those nine months inside nurturing wombs. As a society, we've learned a lot about the importance of prenatal care—but how much do most of us know about *post*natal care? We need a social vision for nurturing childhood as much as we do for nurturing gestation. How different would well-nurtured children look as adults? How would our society look if it were populated by such people?

Seeing childhood as a period of gestation in which children must be protected, nurtured, and supported before they are formally taught facts and cognitive skills is fundamental to the vision of the Outdoor Classroom.

That said, I see the Outdoor Classroom as only one among many elements that are important in serving and supporting children's development. (Others include good parenting, good schooling, and fruitful social activities.) Programs in which the Outdoor Classroom's vision can thrive include programs labeled ECE, child care, day care, preschool, and nursery school. The Outdoor Classroom can be implemented in family child care settings as well.

The Outdoor Classroom: Fulfilling a Vision for Childhood

The Outdoor Classroom's vision is simple: children benefit from spending more time outdoors, especially in natural places. Its goal is equally simple: to increase the quantity, quality, and benefit of outdoor experience for children.

Here is an overview of the key features of the Outdoor Classroom.

The Outdoors Is a Primary Environment for Children

The outdoors is an important learning environment. Learning takes place outdoors that doesn't occur indoors. It is important, then, that outdoor environments be as richly and thoughtfully equipped as indoor ones. Children should be able to move seamlessly between indoors and outdoors; their play and learning should be as easy in one place as the other. Adults should not treat one location as more educational than the other.

Freedom for Children to Play on Their Own

A fundamental principle of the Outdoor Classroom is children's right to initiate their own activities. Children need to explore, imagine, try new things, and learn alone or with friends. Ultimately, what any of us learns most deeply is what we have explored "by ourselves."

Learning Takes Time

Too many adults who work with children try to hurry them. Pressuring children to hurry up inhibits rather than accelerates learning. Like almost everyone else, children learn best when they are relaxed and have open-ended time in which to create their own activities. They need time to refine and anchor new skills. The Outdoor Classroom encourages children to spend as much time as they want outdoors. The *time* children have is often directly related to the *freedom* they have.

Children Need Physical Activity

Physical activity is necessary for children's development and health. Open space offers children opportunities for big movement, vigorous social play, and explorations big and small. Their activities help them refine motor skills and teach them how the world works.

A Full Range of Activities

The Outdoor Classroom believes, "Everything you can do indoors, you can do outdoors, and even more!" Part of the Outdoor Classroom's vision is that indoor and outdoor spaces constitute a single learning environment.

Comprehensive, Holistic, Emergent Curriculum

Curriculum is one of the trickiest elements in ECE. How do we support children's development instead of imposing our own adult agendas on them? In the Outdoor Classroom, we view curriculum as more than an adult-designed course of study or activities. Instead, it is everything that happens during a child's day, everything that a child comes in contact with. Adults observe and respond to children's needs and interests, taking this expanded understanding of curriculum into account.

Engaged Children and Engaged Teachers

Engagement is key to learning. Real learning occurs only when children become engaged with the environment and the people in it, usually through activities that they themselves initiate. Paradoxically, in ECE settings, this means that truly engaged teachers are often in the background, observing and responding rather than leading. Engaged teachers support children who are initiating their own learning.

Developmentally Appropriate Activities

The term *developmentally appropriate* in the Outdoor Classroom means that activities always lie within children's capacity to handle them and are never forced on children. Developmentally appropriate practices are fundamental to effective learning and to the well-being of children.

Moving Beyond This Year's Hot Topic

To the uninformed eye, the Outdoor Classroom may look like nothing more than children playing outside, as children always have. But play in the Outdoor Classroom means something much deeper. And that something is not just the next hot topic, the next new thing. Rather, it is a return to a very old thing: child-centered learning.

The Outdoor Classroom shifts ECE from a primarily indoor, teacher-initiated model to one that embraces outdoor, child-initiated play as critical to children's well-being. By moving children and their activities outdoors, the character and type of what they do are transformed. Children regain control over their activities and become responsible for their own learning and growth, supported by attentive adults who ensure their safety and stimulation. Teachers relinquish control to become observers and supporters.

Reflection

Close your eyes, take a deep breath, and relax. Clear your mind of thoughts. Try to recall the earliest time you can remember being outdoors. Where were you? What were you doing? Who were you with? How did you feel? What did you hear? What did you smell? What did you see? What was the value of that experience? Do children today have similar experiences? Do you think they should?

CHAPTER 1

Children and the Outdoors

A HALF CENTURY AGO, most children had much less structured childhoods than children do today. Whenever I ask audiences about their childhoods, people with gray hair offer remarkably similar stories, whether they grew up in the United States or other countries. They speak of unsupervised summer days, often in natural settings. They were told to "go outside and play." More of them lived in rural areas than children do today. Their neighborhoods were occupied by bands of children who played constantly through backyards or in the streets.

In the small Central Valley town where I grew up in California, most mothers were homemakers and spent little time ferrying children to activities. Instead, we had free-range childhoods. The big exception for me was attending Mrs. Love's—yes, that was really her name!—nursery school at age four for its "socialization opportunities," which also gave my younger brother some time alone with Mom. But Mrs. Love's was not the norm at all: the nation was years away from Head Start, two-working-parent families, and a national vision of preschool as the educational prelude to K–12 public education.

Compared to today's hyperstructured, anxious children, I enjoyed an almost unbelievably unstructured, unsupervised, and—by today's standards—unforgivably unproductive childhood. Just the same, children back then grew up and prospered. The vast majority of us became productive, reasonably well-balanced adults. So what's happened? Why does the childhood of 1950 seem so implausible today?

The answers have profound implications for today's children. And I like to think that the Outdoor Classroom is part of the solution—what needs to change in ECE today.

The Transformation of Risk, Responsibility, and Learning

A half century ago, children were given far more responsibility for their own development. By today's standards, we were exposed to many more risks. Polio was still a fearsome scourge, yet we played and swam together in summer ("polio season"). Cars had no seat belts. Gasoline was leaded. No national playground safety standards existed. For many hours each week, we had no adult supervision. My friends and I took daily risks that could have resulted in injury or even death—we broke bones and incurred cuts, scrapes, and scars; and through trial and error, we learned how to navigate life better. Certainly some of us learned faster than others, but everyone progressed. I don't remember any child dying or even becoming permanently injured from childhood play in my small town. I'm sure that it happened at some point, but it would have been very rare. In our unscripted and largely unsupervised childhoods, we were responsible for a substantial portion of our own welfare and learning.

I'm sure this is why I am always a little startled when I see parents deprive their children of opportunities to learn on their own. Take, for example, a mother who rushes toward a toddler who is taking a tumble before she can even tell if she's needed or if the child can right himself on his own. Rushing to the aid of a fallen toddler is just one example of how adults today deprive children of the opportunity to learn. Falling, after all, is a natural part of learning to walk, and picking oneself up after falling is an important life lesson, both physically and metaphorically. Similarly, scheduling children heavily means they have no time to learn on their own, while restricting their free time to *safe* activities, like playing with electronic devices indoors, deprives them of learning about the world and reinforces the lesson that the world outside is dangerous.

In stark contrast to the 1950s, quiet suburban neighborhoods sit empty on weekends as children stay safely inside or are occupied with tightly-managed outdoor group activities.

The free-range childhood I enjoyed fifty years ago has yielded to one that is highly controlled, heavily scripted, and almost devoid of the considerable benefits of child-initiated, child-controlled activity. Many parents and professionals applaud this shift. If child safety were our only concern, some of these changes might appear relatively benign, even beneficial. But, in fact, the cumulative impact of their unintended, unforeseen consequences is anything but positive. I question whether our children are better off under this much more controlled regime. It seems obvious that scripting every minute of their lives deprives them of important opportunities to learn how to care for themselves.

In gang-infested, inner-city neighborhoods of Southern California where schools are plagued by low test scores and high dropout rates, the reasons for providing tightly controlled, highly scripted childhoods seem compelling: keeping children safe from violence and criminal activity. In nearby high-income enclaves, the rationale is partly the same: keeping children away from drugs and drug dealers, as well as preparing them for success in the best universities and the finest firms. There is no arguing that the world offers new and powerful perils to children today. But imposing unexamined wholesale solutions to life's challenges, such as imposing a blanket restriction on outdoor play, can produce its own set of problems and may reflect an inaccurate perception of real conditions. This was brought home to me when a woman shared her early childhood outdoor experience as part of a large-group sharing time opening one of my presentations on the Outdoor Classroom. She described playing with childhood friends in the streets and alleys of urban Los Angeles. Amazed, I asked if it was really safe for her to do that in a gang-infested neighborhood. Her comment was, "Well, we were street smart." While I recognize that some urban areas have risks, I will never again assume that children can't successfully play there.

The Silent Emergency

The changes we have wrought in childhood in order to protect children from danger constitute a silent emergency. I call it an *emergency* because of the rapidly escalating negative effects it is having on children and society at large. I call it *silent* because the combined impact of several unintended consequences make it so damaging, yet the collective impact of these consequences is rarely discussed or addressed. I believe that the Outdoor Classroom can help early childhood educators address this emergency.

These are the seven most critical issues facing children today that we will discuss here:

1. Lack of exercise

2. Preoccupation with electronic media

3. Perception of outdoors as an unsafe place to play

4. Isolation from and fear of nature

5. Lack of engagement in and connection to the world, including nature

6. Reductive approaches to ECE

7. Epidemic use of behavior-modifying drugs on young children

Lack of Exercise

Lack of exercise and other physical activity is the most glaring of these seven challenges facing our children. It affects children in several ways.

Obesity. Childhood obesity is epidemic in most postindustrial countries, most particularly the United States, in large part because of the dramatic decrease of children's physical play. If you add changes for the

worse in children's eating habits and the quality of the food they consume, the picture is frightening.

Physical development. Early childhood is a critical time in children's physical development. It's the phase in which they build the bodies they'll have for the rest of their lives and establish lifelong habits of physical activity. During their first five years, children are either encouraged or discouraged to be physically active. Their explorations begin with crawling and explode into walking. But not every child is encouraged in these activities. In centers where I worked in East Los Angeles, more than 50 percent of the two- to four-year-olds were diagnosed as at risk for obesity, heart disease, and type 2 diabetes.

Cognitive development. Physical development is the foundation for cognitive development. (Think Piaget and the sensorimotor stage of cognitive development.) From birth, brain development is built on a pattern of physical activity. The greater the frequency and complexity of physical activity, the better it is for brain development. This is particularly important in the first five years of life when most brain growth takes place. Inactivity during this period can be detrimental to a child's cognitive ability in adulthood. Complex (and unstructured) physical activity not only facilitates physical brain development, but it also fosters learning and understanding as children are exposed to a broader range of experience outdoors.

Learning. Lack of physical activity restricts young children's learning because they learn through engaging the world with their senses.

A toddler whose movements are limited by well-meaning adults learns less than one who has greater freedom of movement and more independence. Physical freedom is important to how children develop as learners.

Psychological well-being. The connection between lack of exercise and psychological well-being is probably the most underappreciated challenge children face today. Lack of physical activity and restrictions on vigorous play contribute significantly to children's emotional and mental distress, making it much more difficult for young children to function in structured settings. Some children seem unaffected, but others are permanently damaged in ways that are real if not always readily discernible. Over the thirty years I've operated a child care program, I've enrolled a number of children who had been dismissed from other programs because of so-called behavioral problems. With the emphasis in my program on outdoor activity, all of these children were able to participate successfully, requiring no unusual attention or drugs to modify their behavior.

Preoccupation with Electronic Media

Nothing has made so dramatic a difference in young children's lives as the near-ubiquity of electronic media. Today children are drowning in it. Television has become a 24/7 vendor of every conceivable form of entertainment, with multiple channels targeted directly at children. In fall 2009, Matea Gold reported new findings by Nielsen:

> The amount of television usage by children reached an eight-year high, with kids ages 2 to 5 watching the screen for more than 32 hours a week on average and those ages 6 to 11 watching more than 28 hours. The analysis, based on the fourth quarter of 2008, measured children's consumption of live and recorded TV, as well as VCR and game console usage. (*Los Angeles Times*, October 27, 2009)

The electronic silo. The *Los Angeles Times* report did not take into account traveling media, such as DVD players in cars or handheld devices, which the Nielsen ratings do not track. The steady increase in these powerful handheld devices represents perhaps the most insidious and transformative change in early childhood. Like all technologies, such devices can be used to connect or to isolate us—it all depends on your point of reference. But without adult intervention, these devices travel everywhere with children, in effect surrounding them with an electronic silo that seals them away from family and environment. The use of handheld devices eats away at the time young children could be spending on learning how to conduct interpersonal relationships face-to-face or interacting physically with the environment around them.

When children become focused on electronic media, they give up activities that have formed the backbone of early childhood development throughout history. These activities are nonsedentary, multifaceted, and interrelated; they provide all that is necessary for healthy, optimal development. They include the following:

- playing outdoors

- engaging in high levels of unstructured physical activity

- physically manipulating large and small objects

- playing physically with others: building and maintaining relationships

- communicating with others face-to-face

- taking personal responsibility

- solving problems

- exploring and learning how the world works

While media-driven activities may resemble those on this list, they are fundamentally different in what they involve and what they produce. A high level of physical activity is one obvious difference; one of the most damaging effects of media addiction is the amount of sedentary indoor time children now spend, which frequently results in increased body weight. Time spent on media replaces time spent outdoors on physical activities.

Poor health is only the first of the deficits that results from media-dominated early childhoods. Face-to-face, hands-on, real-time physical activities cannot be replaced or replicated by electronic devices. The more time children spend in virtual worlds, the less time they spend in the real one, learning about it. The more that children believe virtual worlds are real, the less they understand how the real world actually works. Learning about the world through electronic media warps children's sense of personal responsibility and gives them a false sense of power, cause and effect, and consequence. Loss of face-to-face interactions prevents children from learning how to be human and how to relate to other humans. When children do not learn to dwell fully within the present, real-time, physical moment, they often suffer behavioral and academic difficulties that can have profound short- and long-term impacts.

Impact on brain function and attention. Watching TV affects brain function. The American Academy of Pediatricians (AAP) recommends that children under two not watch TV. In 2007, the AAP summarized the results of its study in an article titled "Early TV Viewing Habits Could Have Lasting Effect on Kids' Attention":

> Children who watch more television in their early years may be more likely to have attention problems as teens. In a study from the University of Otago, in Dunedin, New Zealand, more than 1,000 children were observed from age 3 through age 15. . . . For every additional 50 minutes of television watched on average per day, there was a measurable negative impact on attention. Those who watched the most TV earlier in childhood were more likely to have attention problems. In particular, those children who watched more than two hours per day had above-average symptoms of attention difficulties in adolescence. . . . Possible explanations may be the world portrayed on television makes real-life tasks seem boring in comparison, or that watching TV displaces the activities that encourage attention such as reading and playing games. (AAP 2007)

Much of the commentary on this issue focuses on the mesmerizing effects of watching TV and the passive nature of this activity. Young children need to be mentally and physically active in order to develop adequately.

Perception of Outdoors as an Unsafe Place to Play

Compared to those of previous generations, the lives of children of all socioeconomic levels today are more constrained. In the 1990s, studies in the United Kingdom found that the space around a home in which a child could roam and play freely had shrunk to one-ninth what it had been only twenty years earlier (Tovey 2007). Many factors contribute to this trend, but the key one may be parents' fear of what could happen to their unsupervised children.

The world is clearly different from that of the mid-twentieth century. Nevertheless, statistics do not support the common perception that children are now at greater risk. What they do support is that

when something happens to a child today, parents are much more aware of it because of the pervasiveness of media reportage. Perception drives personal reality and behavior—and inundated by repeated recountings of abductions and murders of children, parents have succumbed to their fears and altered their and their children's behavior. Children no longer have much control over their own play; they are herded to regulated activities that run them and their parents ragged. Organized sports, arts, tutoring, playdates, and the like are the socially correct choices today. Having time to oneself, playing outdoors with friends, or venturing into "the wild" are forbidden.

This shift comes at a high cost. Children no longer are given enough freedom to cultivate the skills they need to function successfully in an unpredictable world.

When children are shuttled through a series of highly structured, fairly predictable activities instead, many learning opportunities are missed.

Isolation from and Fear of Nature

Over the last several decades, children have become increasingly isolated from and fearful of nature. Again, popular media bear significant responsibility. Nature is often characterized as weather-related disasters, jogger-attacking mountain lions, or coyotes that carry off toddlers. Families spend less time outdoors because of the electronic diversions available to them; these seem safer than taking or allowing their children outdoors.

Such fears are extensions of media-driven fears in urban and suburban neighborhoods about leaving the house. Powerful as these unsupported perceptions can be, they can be trumped by positive, real-life experience.

One parent told me how difficult she had found it to choose between taking her children to a theme park or a mountain retreat. No fear factor entered into her consideration of the theme park; the activities there would be predictable and safe. Going to the mountains, however, evoked a range of fears about attacks by wild animals and children injuring themselves. She was also worried by what she described as "not knowing what we'd do up there for an entire three-day weekend." Nevertheless,

she chose the mountain retreat. After they arrived and unloaded the car, her children broke for the surrounding forest and its fallen logs, rocks to climb, and an infinite number of things to pick up and examine. The mother's immediate, knee-jerk reaction was to control the situation: "Be careful! Don't do that! Look out! Get out of there!" Quickly exhausted, she fell into a worried silence while her children successfully mastered one self-appointed task after another, incurring only an occasional scratch or scape, none of which bothered them at all. After the family had eaten, the mother wandered back outside under the starlit sky. Looking up, she thought, "This is so much more beautiful than an amusement park."

Children gravitate to nature naturally when they're given the opportunity, but their attitudes and behaviors are usually formed by those of the adults around them. Cultivating a love of and connection with nature requires the active involvement of adults. In the case I've described, the children were lucky because their mother, though skeptical, was willing to give nature a chance. Many children are faced with adults who themselves have no connection with nature—or worse, an active aversion to it.

Lack of Engagement in and Connection to the World, Including Nature

Humans need to understand cause-and-effect relationships and complex interactions in order to make intelligent, life-affirming choices. Isolation, separation, and narrow worldviews inhibit the development of these skills. Here again, the media has proven to be a double-edged sword. While it often provides in-depth information, it also promotes simplistic worldviews that ignore or misinterpret important facts.

Human survival depends on learning to address complexity and to acknowledge the consequences of one's own actions. Our society's collective failure to do so has resulted in some of our most serious political, social, economic, and environmental problems. Children need to learn these humane skills from a very early age, and they are dependent on adults for guidance in learning them.

While they need adults to inform them and model appropriate behavior, in the end children learn to address complexity and acknowledge consequences by communicating with others, working on

projects collectively, problem solving, and observing the world around them. They need support in developing patience and environments in which they can learn about cause and effect, hypothesize, and test their ideas.

Reductive Approaches to ECE

Instead of giving children the complex education they need, many learning programs today seem fueled by media-inspired fear and the comforts of predictability. They have increasingly narrowed the focus of education for young children to a single goal: serving the objectives of primary school. The broad, holistic approach that was ECE's hallmark for decades has been sacrificed in many programs to the much narrower goal of supposedly preparing children for kindergarten.

Like nature, educational environments should be inspiring and stimulating. If they are instead like electronic media—narrow in range, rigid in the interactions they make possible—the rich potential of each child for curiosity and exploration will not be tapped. Focusing almost exclusively on children's mental acuity also puts them at social and emotional risk. Approximately 11 percent of American children attempt suicide by age eighteen; it is impossible to ignore the role that our narrow educational system plays in their lack of well-being (McElroy 2011).

Epidemic Use of Behavior-Modifying Drugs on Young Children

Consider these statistics:

- Amphetamines are the most commonly prescribed medications for children (Larson 2011).

- In 2002, the number of American children ages two to eighteen who were being prescribed antidepressants had increased fivefold since 1995 (St. Luke's Health Initiatives 2006).

- Between 2000 and 2003, psychotropic drug utilization in preschoolers increased by 49 percent. For the first time, spending on such drugs surpassed spending on antibiotics and asthma medications for children (Medco Health Solutions 2004).

- Eight million American children are on prescribed drugs for behavioral or learning difficulties (St. Luke's Health Initiatives 2006).

While the US government wages its war on drugs, physicians are prescribing drugs to huge numbers of children. The crucial question is "Why?" Is there something wrong with children today? Attention deficit hyperactivity disorder (ADHD) was largely undiagnosed fifty years ago. Were there that many untreated children back then? Are children born less healthy today?

Discussion of these questions, particularly in relation to attention deficit disorder (ADD) and ADHD, is animated. Speculation runs broad and deep and includes the roles of artificial additives to food, pesticides, and genetics. Multiple contributing factors are likely—but one of them, prescribed drugs, is not frequently considered.

When a child functions poorly at school, most people assume that he has a problem. This is a one-sided way of looking at the situation, and it is based on a long history of viewing children as lacking uniqueness and fundamental rights—children should not influence the educational system in which they are placed; they should simply deal with it. In earlier times, such beliefs were reflected in the physical force used against children who misbehaved or failed to perform adequately. Today we use drugs. However, this need not be the case. Often the symptoms that are treated by drugs can either be prevented or treated in ways that are more effective and have fewer side effects than drugs. For example, children can be placed in less rigid, more supportive educational programs.

Responding to the Silent Emergency

Programs of ECE and care are uniquely positioned to address the full array of the silent emergency's challenges and more. Early childhood education programs are required to have outdoor play yards. Through implementation of the Outdoor Classroom in those play yards, the silent emergency can be addressed effectively.

1. **Lack of exercise.** Just getting children outdoors increases the likelihood that they will become more physically active. They should be able to move indoors and outdoors freely much of the day.

The more time they spend outside, the more active they will probably be. That said, other factors play significant roles in increasing children's physical activity: the teacher's skill and engagement, the design of outdoor spaces, the program's structure. Children, rather than adults, should structure their own playtime and provide their own motivation. The Outdoor Classroom encourages development of lifelong patterns of healthy physical activity.

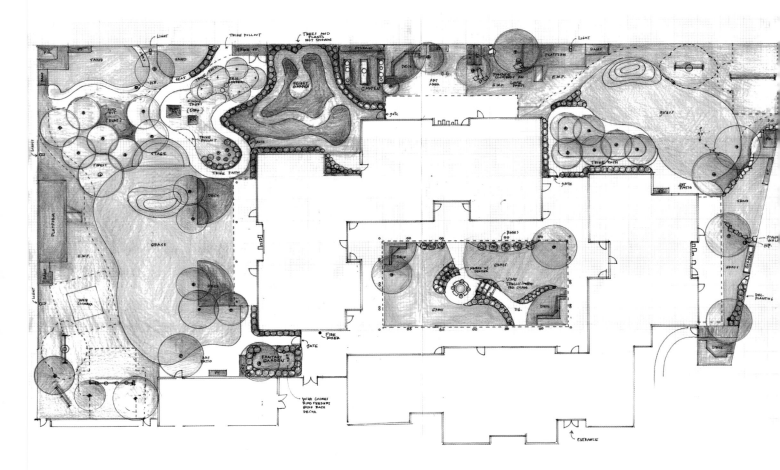

2. **Preoccupation with electronic media.** The time children spend with media is time not spent outdoors. Fortunately, ECE programs can offer children the opportunity for physically active, hands-on, face-to-face activities with other people. These activities should involve "loose parts" that children can manipulate. The loose parts can be large, requiring plenty of full-body exertion and coordination to move (for example, logs, branches, large waffle blocks, milk crates), or small. Activities can include art, music, blocks, reading, and writing. They should include face-to-face interactions and group problem solving, like group projects and games and affinity group activities. The natural environment can be used to engage children in hands-on science and math experiences. The Outdoor Classroom's goal for outdoor time is to deepen children's connection to and love of the outdoors and counter the pull of electronics.

3. **Lack of a safe space to play outside.** In the past, the outdoors was an immensely rich environment for children to play in as they chose. Now that children's free movement outside their homes is much more constrained, ECE play yards have sometimes become the only outdoor sanctuaries in which children can play. Because these spaces have become replacements for broader outdoor experiences for many children, it is important that they reproduce some of the features of those freer, now-lost experiences: they should offer children opportunities to learn how to handle useful risks successfully—for example, climbing, digging, and jumping. At the same time, children should be protected from risks that are not developmentally beneficial, such as exposure to pollution, traffic, and random encounters with strangers.

4. **Isolation from and fear of nature.** Helping children to connect to nature is one of the great missed opportunities in most ECE play yards. These spaces should be designed and constructed as much as possible to replicate rich, natural environments. The natural features of the yards should teach children about nature through direct, hands-on contact. Teachers should help children learn stewardship of our natural environment by encouraging them to care for at least some aspect of the yard, such as the garden.

5. **Lack of engagement in and connection to the world, including nature.** A critical task for children is learning about cause and effect—how the world works. A child's intelligence matures by moving from a simple, emotionally driven worldview to one that accepts and enjoys complexity and draws upon facts. Although refining these skills is a lifelong process, it is at its greatest intensity during early childhood. Outdoor environments and outdoor play strongly support this development, because they teach children increasingly complex lessons about cause and effect. These lessons, in turn, become lifelong behaviors and help children master the challenges they face later in life.

6. **Reductive approaches to ECE.** The current ECE emphasis on preparing children for school tends to make programs teacher-directed rather than child-centered. The Outdoor Classroom helps to restore the traditional ECE focus on the whole child. It emphasizes socioemotional and physical development by encouraging children to take the lead in developing and implementing their own activities. Children's emotional maturity and social skills are considered as important as their ability to tell the difference between a letter and a number. This approach lays a more complete foundation for school readiness and fosters joy in learning, which is a critical factor in school success.

Another valuable element of holistic ECE is its support of children's psychological well-being. Children who are not emotionally healthy are not as prepared for the rigor of academic programs or as advanced in the socioemotional development needed for success in school. The Outdoor Classroom provides rich physical and program environments in which all children can develop a strong sense of self. Their self-directed play helps them develop the skills they need to navigate the learning and social environments of kindergarten and elementary school.

7. **Epidemic use of behavior-modifying drugs on young children.**
The Outdoor Classroom places lighter demands on conformity in activities than programs that are teacher directed. What role structured programs play in demands that children be placed on behavior-modifying drugs is not clear, but I can say that the Outdoor Classroom allows children across a broad spectrum of behavioral styles to be successful. I have observed dramatic drops in conflicts, declines in challenging behaviors, and greater success for children, indoors and out, in programs with this approach.

I witnessed the power of the Outdoor Classroom to benefit an "active learner" during a site visit. The center had previously allowed

children only a half hour outdoors and had recently doubled that time to an hour while greatly enriching its activity centers. One boy—I'll call him Jimmy—caught my eye. When he first burst outside, he went straight to a Lego table and began constructing a tower. The noise from children playing soccer quickly drew him away. Just as quickly, a girl sat down at his place and began to work on his abandoned tower. The teacher intervened and said, "That's Jimmy's, and he'll be back." Sure enough, five or six minutes later, he returned to the tower, only to leave again when the noise from another activity drew him away.

This sequence repeated itself five or six times, ending when Jimmy completed a large and complex tower in the company of other boys. Jimmy was a classic active learner who needed a flexible schedule to complete his quiet fine-motor task. The Outdoor Classroom provided this. Jimmy's teacher reported that after the longer outdoor periods had been introduced, the children performed better indoors: they were quieter, more focused, and more productive.

The seven-part silent emergency identifies how the Outdoor Classroom addresses some key challenges facing children today, improves the condition of children in ECE, and helps to restore the power and joy of childhood. In the next chapter, I will examine what the Outdoor Classroom requires of adults who implement its practices.

Summary

Childhood has changed dramatically over the past half century. The natural opportunity children had to develop by employing their own initiative in an independent setting has mostly gone away. Children are additionally faced with a silent emergency of challenges never before imagined:

1. Lack of exercise

2. Preoccupation with electronic media

3. Perception of outdoors as an unsafe place to play

4. Isolation from and fear of nature

5. Lack of engagement in and connection to the world, including nature

6. Reductive approaches to ECE

7. Epidemic use of behavior-modifying drugs on young children

The Outdoor Classroom helps to restore the traditional benefits of childhood while addressing these challenges:

1. Getting children outside and more active

2. Involving children in hands-on, loose-parts outdoor play

3. Creating opportunities to learn how to handle outdoor risks safely

4. Connecting children to nature in ways that encourage them to connect more deeply

5. Teaching children about cause and effect through outdoor and interpersonal activities

6. Providing children with a wide range of activities that support their holistic development

Reflection

Quickly evaluate your existing outdoor program and play yard. Which of the approaches suggested in chapter 1 are you using? How can you enhance them? Which strategies are you not using? How can you implement them?

CHAPTER 2

Working with Children in the Outdoor Classroom

WORKING WITH CHILDREN in outdoor environments requires a different set of skills and knowledge than indoor settings. The people designing such sites need to understand how children grow, learn, and use outdoor environments. They also need to understand how early childhood education (ECE) programs work. In addition, they must understand the design, construction, functions, and landscaping of outdoor spaces. Obviously, no one person needs all of these skills. For example, those of you who are teachers need to know enough about landscaping to provide useful input to landscape architects about planting and gardening to create meaningful outdoor programs, and enough about natural environments to support children's learning. Contractors need to know what children are capable of at different ages, how to protect them from unacceptable risks, and how to build sufficient challenges into play yards. Every member of the team designing an Outdoor Classroom needs to communicate effectively with the others.

In this chapter, I'll examine the three linchpins holding together the Outdoor Classroom: teaching, program design, and environment. I'll also review how prospective Outdoor Classroom participants can work together effectively.

Teachers' Shifting Roles

Adults working with children in the Outdoor Classroom are embarking on their own journeys. These start with the conviction that ECE works *within* childhood, not simply with it. Their path departs from some ECE programs because it is grounded in the belief that childhood is not something that adults should control but instead something that adults must remain mindful of and attuned and responsive to. In effect, adults must be able to re-enter childhood and work from within it. In ECE, the best teachers understand and feel what children feel and respond from there. Most of them accomplish this by drawing upon their own childhood experiences, something that is often called *connecting with their own inner child.* This is not the same as knowing intellectually how children behave; it is being emotionally connected to children and being skilled enough to work with them from that emotional place.

Working with children stimulates memories and feelings of our own childhoods. We can use what we feel to work more effectively with children. But we can do so only if we value each child. We cannot protect, nurture, educate, and support someone we do not value.

Overview of Skills and Qualities

Many of the skills and qualities needed by teachers working in the Outdoor Classroom are the same ones needed while working indoors. But some skills and concepts that are used outdoors are not commonly taught:

- thinking about the outdoors as a classroom

- working in a natural environment

- facilitating indoor-outdoor flow

- working with children outdoors

- engaging engaged children

- developing outdoor programs

- evaluating, designing, and modifying outdoor environments

Thinking about the Outdoors as a Classroom

Traditional ECE training does not include thinking about the outdoors as a classroom space. So your first and probably most important step should be to drop old notions about the outdoors as simply a space for children to use during recess. Think instead about indoor and outdoor classrooms as different only in their floors, walls, and ceilings. You don't have to remove your teacher's hat when you move outdoors. Continue to be a teacher, and work with just as much focus as you did indoors. Your role is not to become a playground monitor, and outdoor time is not

simply a break from more important matters. Outdoor activities promote just as much learning as indoor ones and require just as much of your thought and attention.

Teachers need to drop the belief that outdoor activity is purely play and not as important as what takes place indoors. You need to think of play as learning; all curriculums should be play based. Recognize and make use of the unique opportunities for learning that are available outdoors.

Working in a Natural Environment

Teaching outdoors isn't the same as teaching indoors. You will need a slightly different attitude and a different way of working with children. First of all, you will need to accommodate the weather. Depending on conditions outdoors, this may mean big or small changes. In any case, weather itself has a lot to teach children, so be enthusiastic about it; turn it into something teachable. At the very least, you need to be *committed* to being outdoors. Remember these two things: first, children usually want to go outside, and second, they are strongly influenced by your attitude. It's critical to maintain a positive attitude about being outdoors in all sorts of weather.

Moving outdoors doesn't necessarily mean that you'll be moving into a natural environment. In some ECE play yards, weather and an

occasional bird, insect, or rodent may be the only natural features you'll find; concrete and asphalt hardscapes are all too common. Assess the outdoor environment of your ECE program. Where it lacks natural features, find ways to modify and enrich the environment.

Where the environment is mostly natural, you need to know how to work with it and be able to answer children's questions about it. Here is knowledge you'll need:

- fundamental understanding of plants and wild animals, growth and decay, natural cycles, and ecology

- gardening skills

- ability to help children explore and learn in a natural environment

- skill in setting up activities in a natural environment

- knowledge about cultivating, maintaining, and enhancing a natural environment

Working with Children Outdoors

Working outdoors with children is different because the space is larger and has a different nature (pun intended). Outdoors, children should be less controlled and directed by adults. They can engage in more complex and less structured activities. This doesn't mean they're out of control— it means that when they are deeply engaged, they are focused, happy, and peaceful, even when very energetic.

Because outdoor play is so open ended, teachers are often puzzled about their own role in it. Given that today such an issue is made of children's safety, many teachers decide that their role is to control children's actions to ensure that no one gets hurt. Such thinking fails to distinguish between supervision and control; it often takes the form of telling children what to do—including how to play. While this may make children safer in the short term, in the long run, it increases their risk because it fails to give them opportunities to manage their own risks successfully. Children who aren't given the chance to learn how to manage themselves often get into trouble as soon as a teacher isn't present. That's hard on the child and hard on you.

Ideally, you will behave toward children as an engaged teacher. This is a skill you can learn and refine through practice. It's a key element in the Outdoor Classroom, and it involves so many instinctive steps that neither you nor an observer is probably even aware of most of them. Nonetheless, understanding engagement is critical to working more successfully with children.

Engaging Engaged Children

Engaging children is the primary objective of the Outdoor Classroom. Engagement doesn't happen by accident; it requires the support of teachers on many levels. You need to support children's initiative, provide them with physical resources, and participate in ways that help them connect with activities successfully so they can expand their own learning.

Teachers' engagement includes many steps:

1. awareness
2. observation
3. connection
4. reception
5. acceptance
6. alignment
7. empathy
8. unconditional positive regard
9. understanding
10. presence
11. communication
12. action
13. reflection
14. evaluation
15. learning

To engage effectively as a teacher, you need to understand these concepts:

- Delivery is part of the content.
- The method is the lesson.
- The environment is a teacher.

Delivery is part of the content. Children don't learn only the content they're taught—they learn from the way that content is delivered. In *The Courage to Teach,* Parker J. Palmer introduces the concept he calls "you teach who you are." As a teacher, you can be more important than the content you are teaching. Teachers are models, and young children learn by emulating models. They may not always understand the content you are offering them, but they do understand the tone and the manner in which you communicate it. Psychologist and educator Mary Hulnick expresses this another way: she says that when we communicate with each other, the energy our communication rides on is just as important—or more so—than its content. We communicate not just with words but with attitudes, emotions, physicality, and intent. These forms of expression convey meaning that each of us interprets based on our own understanding.

The method is the lesson. Teachers are only part of the education system. The style of the program or curriculum is another. When children must sit and listen to their teacher, they learn several largely unspoken lessons:

- The teacher is in charge of learning.
- I must sit still to learn.
- I must listen to the teacher to learn.
- What the teacher says is all I need to know.

If the teaching method requires children to repeat what you have said or to say what you affirm is the correct answer, children learn that copying the teacher is how they learn. They also tend to take on negative self-images:

- I can't learn on my own.
- I can't move and learn at the same time.
- My own thoughts are not valuable.
- I am wrong if I am not copying the teacher.

The messages children receive about themselves and formal learning from traditional teaching methods have profound, lifelong effects. Children who do not fit in are labeled negatively. These labels tend to stick throughout their schooling and become self-fulfilling prophecies. Children who don't work well within conventional classrooms may be termed *poor learners* when they simply learn differently or at a different pace.

The environment is a teacher. Physical environments teach children. For this reason, it is important to create environments that tell children they are valued, that show them what learning environments look and feel like. Different learning methods require different environments. Placing children at individual desks says something different than gathering them in a group around a table. Round rooms read to the eye differently than square ones. Classrooms without windows affect children differently than ones with windows.

Not surprisingly, the Outdoor Classroom represents a paradigm shift in several ways: it supports a much broader range of engagement, allows a much wider range of activities, and supports more opportunities for self-directed learning.

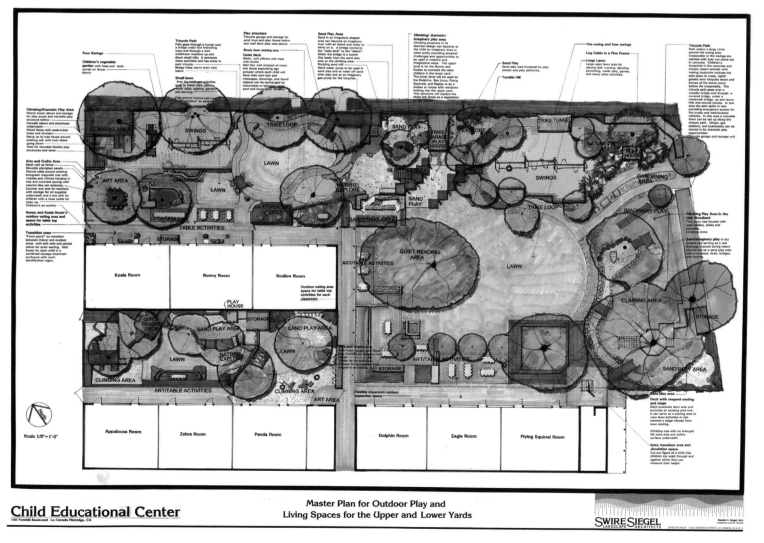

Child Educational Center
140 Foothill Boulevard La Cañada Flintridge, CA

Master Plan for Outdoor Play and
Living Spaces for the Upper and Lower Yards

SWIRE SIEGEL
LANDSCAPE ARCHITECTS

Teachers' Roles

To support the Outdoor Classroom fully, teachers need to understand some new roles. The role models of many ECE teachers are the previous generation of traditionalists who practiced teacher-directed learning. This is going to be different; you're going to be wearing other caps. Let's look at some of your new roles:

Monitor. You're going to be replacing the role of supervisor with that of monitor. A monitor doesn't simply watch over things: instead, you measure the level and nature of activities and, when necessary, trigger a response. This role is especially challenging in the Outdoor Classroom because outdoor environments offer much more complexity, challenge, and risk to children.

Intervener/adjudicator/protector. Making sure that children remain safe is a complex skill. When you intervene, you step in as the adult in charge and take action based on your assessment of what is needed. Intervention looks quite different in teacher-directed and child-centered programs. In the former, interventions are often undertaken to reassert a teacher's control. In the latter, interventions focus on teaching children how to handle conflicts or danger so they can control situations on their own. As an adjudicator, you mediate disputes and teach children how to resolve their own conflicts.

Teachers always try to protect children from danger, whether it's self-generated or caused by others. But here, too, there's a difference in how you protect children in teacher-directed and child-centered programs. In the former, teachers are more likely to "just say no" when danger is imminent. In child-centered programs, if a child engages in risky

behavior, you take the time to help him understand the risk and, if possible, help him develop enough skill to engage in the activity safely.

Because outdoor environments offer so many risks and opportunities to children, implementing the Outdoor Classroom may require you to broaden what you regard as acceptable activity so children can master what the outdoors offers them. Traditional programs restrict children by denying them the opportunities and risks that the outdoors provides.

Facilitator. Every teacher is a facilitator, but as an ECE teacher who is implementing the Outdoor Classroom, you use your skills as a facilitator to support children's natural talents and abilities and to help them use those to become their own best teachers. Facilitating in this way calls upon several subroles.

Information provider. The Outdoor Classroom teacher observes children at play and provides information based on their questions or what you think they need to further their learning. The information you provide is not based on a lesson plan but on what the children are doing. Great care is taken to be conservative in your information sharing so as not to short-circuit the children's natural talent for developing information on their own through their own initiative and learning process.

Mentor/guide. As a mentor/guide, you observe children and make your contribution in as low-key a way as possible, allowing the children to lead. You don't tell them what to do or how to do it. Instead, you encourage them to figure things out themselves and you assist them as active learners. Mentor/guides are always available when children need a supportive adult.

Provocateur. As a teacher, you model inquisitiveness and encourage children to expand their thinking by posing "What if?" questions.

Supporter/supplier. You ensure a supportive physical environment and enough supplies so children can embark on great learning adventures and activities. You see to it that the Outdoor Classroom has adequate storage for supplies and that children can obtain them without much help from adults.

Program organizer/designer. Designing and organizing the Outdoor Classroom's child-centered environment should focus on supporting independent play and learning rather than a teacher-determined curriculum.

Developing and Implementing Programs for the Outdoor Classroom

Programs include a number of facets:

- philosophy and approach
- curriculum and content
- implementation of activities

Philosophy and Approach

A key objective of the Outdoor Classroom is helping children become independent learners. The Outdoor Classroom supports children while they develop and carry out their own activities. Doing so teaches them creativity, responsibility, cooperation, and communication as well as the particular lessons of specific activities.

Curriculum and Content

The Outdoor Classroom's fundamental premise about curriculum is "Anything that is done inside can be done outside." Simple as this sounds, it represents a big paradigm shift for many programs. It isn't easy, for example, for a teacher-directed program to shift to a child-centered one that uses two to five times as much space as its indoor classroom. However, the simplest approach is to begin by moving what you have inside outside. You read indoors, so read outdoors. Children write indoors, so let them write outdoors. Children do puzzles indoors, and they can do them outdoors. While the content of activities can be the same, the way in which the curriculum is implemented will usually require a little tweaking. You may need a blanket and basket to create a reading area. You might provide clipboards for writing. Puzzles on outdoor tables may need a drop cloth placed underneath to catch falling pieces. With these usually minor adaptations, everything is possible.

Emergent curriculum. The Outdoor Classroom can work harmoniously with other curricular approaches if they are not rigid or narrow. Emergent curriculums are compatible with the Outdoor Classroom because they reflect children's interests and needs; in both cases, children develop most of the ideas they work with while you and other adults support them by asking questions, responding to children's inquiries, and supporting their interests.

Preparing children for traditional school environments. The Outdoor Classroom supports preschool children regardless of the kind of kindergarten program they will enter. I know it does so successfully because its approach works well beyond children's preschool years. Many elementary schools have expressed an interest in the Outdoor Classroom and have implemented some of its elements. Children who have learned in Outdoor Classrooms are successful in elementary school.

A few years after we opened our Outdoor Classroom program and a few classes of children had gone on to kindergarten, we asked their kindergarten teachers if our children could be identified as having come from our program. With some degree of trepidation we heard, "Oh yes, we certainly know the Outdoor Classroom children." Catastrophic thoughts ran through my head—but she continued, "We can identify those children out on the playground; they are the children who are solving their own problems without having to come to a teacher for help. Even more, those children are helping other children solve their problems without having to ask for teacher assistance."

The behaviors and skills this anecdote describes are critical for success in kindergarten. The Outdoor Classroom provides a broad, comprehensive foundation that prepares children well for school success.

Despite this fact, some teachers are reluctant to implement the Outdoor Classroom because of the demands that will be placed on children to reach certain achievement levels when they enter kindergarten. They assume (incorrectly) that children cannot be adequately prepared through the Outdoor Classroom. They're wrong on multiple counts: every skill required in kindergarten can be learned in the program. The Outdoor Classroom develops character and teaches skills that help children become successful in school and later life. The Outdoor Classroom teaches things that can't be readily learned indoors.

Implementation of Activities

Implementation is key to the Outdoor Classroom program, and it's shared between teachers and children. Those of you who are teachers bring your understanding of child development, curriculum design, learning theory, and the wisdom of experience; children bring their drive and enthusiasm, their energy for exploring, adventuring, practicing, and questioning.

The Outdoor Classroom thrives when teachers focus on learning and growth objectives, help children acquire the knowledge and skills they need to reach their destinations, and encourage them to learn. Children fuel activities and choose short-term directions.

Designing and Working with Environments for the Outdoor Classroom

As an early childhood teacher, you should have a basic understanding of the environment used by the Outdoor Classroom, just as you should know something about indoor design. Such knowledge helps you work effectively in those settings, evaluate how they work, and make improvements. Learn about these elements of the Outdoor Classroom's setting:

- site and climate
- natural features
- general layout
- storage
- basic design details
- basic maintenance of environment

Site and Climate

Early childhood educators are often unaware of the hazards just outside the play yard's fence. Such hazards include cars on the street or in parking lots adjacent to the yard. Less visible hazards include overhanging trees, dangerous human activities, hazardous-waste storage, utility lines, and more. Each of these can pose an immediate or occasional threat under certain conditions, such as storms, earthquakes, or nearby construction. As a teacher, you should monitor such risks, seek to minimize them, and alter activity in the Outdoor Classroom when necessary.

You should also be familiar with weather patterns throughout the year:

- prevailing winds
- patterns of shade
- temperature variations
- average monthly precipitation
- cyclical weather events (for example, thunderstorms, tornadoes, hurricanes, straight-line winds)
- short-term weather forecasts

Knowing these patterns helps you schedule short-term activities and make long-term decisions about outdoor design and construction. Knowing short-term weather forecasts is particularly important in planning outdoor activities and devising back-up alternatives.

Implementing the Outdoor Classroom in Challenging Climates

Every time I make a presentation outside of Southern California (and even sometimes there!) someone comments along the following lines, "Well, the Outdoor Classroom is easy to do in Southern California where the weather is always nice, but what about in (fill in the location) in (fill in the season)? How do you implement it there, then?" The truth is that Southern California does have fair weather much of the time. It is also true that every location has challenging weather, even Southern California. In many places, winters are very cold and snowy. Summers can be very hot and humid. In some places, it is very windy year-round. Some regions are prone to short-term dramatic conditions such as hurricanes, tornadoes, heavy rain, and even earthquakes.

No matter the location and climate, the philosophy, principles, and practices of the Outdoor Classroom still apply. What changes is the way in which they are implemented. There are both opportunities and challenges to be found in a harsher climate. So children in the north of Scotland build castles from ice. Children in Norway learn early how to travel on skis. Children in Oklahoma play outside when temperatures are in the 90s and the humidity is dripping wet, while the teachers gamely keep up. (I saw a little boy from the Cherokee Nation trot happily barefooted on pea gravel in 100° F midday sun—perhaps an ECE version of the "fire walk.")

The most common reality is that most children love to go outdoors whenever possible. There may be challenges of clothing, preparation, transition, and cleanup, but as is said in the colder climes, "There is no such thing as bad weather, just bad clothing." If the teachers are enthusiastic, creative, and dedicated, the Outdoor Classroom can be a reality everywhere for much of the year.

Natural Features

As a teacher, you should have basic knowledge about the natural features of your Outdoor Classroom. These include the following:

Hazards. Natural features can be hazardous to small children, so you need to assess probable risks. For example, mulberry leaves can be poisonous if eaten in large quantities, but because children are unlikely to eat very many, mulberry trees should be allowed in play yards. Other hazards present more ambiguous trade-offs. Roses have thorns, and three- and four-year-olds can prick themselves on them. Should roses then be banned from play yards? Perhaps a better solution is to teach children how to treat bushes with thorns—carefully close up, or simply from a respectful distance. How about trees with branches that break easily, like silver maples? Their breakage is not something children can be taught to avoid, so such trees are not recommended for preschool play yards. You'll learn about these hazards one by one.

The frequently planted oleander is poisonous and never suitable for children's environments.

Trees. Teachers should know the trees in their play yards, know whether they shed leaves or branches, and know how the trees can support children's activities.

Grass. Teachers should know where selected grasses grow best and what varieties hold up best to underfoot traffic.

Plants. Teachers should be aware of the poisonous plants in their area as well as plants that can provide learning opportunities for children. Poisonous plants should never be permitted in any play yard used by young children.

Soils. Teachers should know enough about the soil in the play yard to understand if water from precipitation and irrigation can drain effectively. Soil and drainage affect how well grass and other plants can grow.

Animals. Teachers should be familiar with the insects and other animals that inhabit the yard and the trees and grounds surrounding it. Assessing the hazards that diseases carried by wild animals may pose is important. Teach children about these hazards without making them afraid of animals. You can encourage the safe presence of wild animals by putting out birdbaths and salt licks that children can view from a distance.

General Layout

Teachers need to understand how activity areas should be laid out. The layout should reflect the natural environment of the site, including climate and site-related hazards. General layout should factor in the relationship of the yard to the building and how children flow between the two.

Storage

Teachers should have a clear idea about what kind of storage sustains outdoor activities. Storage should be located in places that can be easily accessed by both teachers and children so that both are supported in outdoor activities.

Basic Design Details

Design details make a huge difference in how well a play yard functions. Teachers need a fundamental understanding of design details to prevent hazards to children, minimize impediments, and enhance children's activities. These details include type of wood used in decks, edge finishes on concrete, size of overhangs on patios, and type of borders on sand boxes.

Basic Maintenance of the Environment

Play yards often suffer from poor maintenance. Teachers need to know what kinds of maintenance are needed and on what schedule they should be performed. You and the children should be partly responsible for maintaining the outdoor classroom, just as you are for the indoor classroom. Having children participate in maintaining their outdoor play space teaches them responsibility and stewardship.

Teachers should be aware of safety and health; wear and tear on furniture, toys, equipment, and buildings; condition of the natural environment; and condition of human-made improvements. You should report anything in need of repair to administrators. Be persistent, because some administrators may procrastinate in dealing with these problems because they do not have to deal with them on a daily basis. Maintenance issues become critical when children's well-being is at risk.

How much maintenance should you and the children be responsible for? Other than directly supporting children's activities and meeting their needs, you should not perform maintenance that can be handled by yard and/or custodial staff. You are not a custodian or a maintenance person. Outdoor environments should be designed, built, and maintained so teachers are not required to undertake maintenance. A common example of poor design is placement of concrete walkways or patios next to areas containing sand. Teachers often end up spending too much time sweeping sand from concrete to remove slipping hazards.

On the other hand, you and the children can contribute to keeping the environment in good shape and participating meaningfully in its care. For example, you can make sure that fall pads, blankets, and play equipment are not left on the grass so long that grass dies. You and the children should be responsible for activity gardens, garden boxes, and pots that are part of the program's curriculum. Children should help with permanent features of the play yard by raking leaves or pulling weeds, as long as doing so is not the primary way the environment is maintained, but rather a teaching or play activity.

Summary

Teaching, program design, and environment contribute to defining the quality of your Outdoor Classroom experience. You need traditional teaching skills, but you also need other skills for working outdoors. The key to success is effectively engaging and supporting children in their activities. Toward this end, you must play a variety of roles. To take advantage of the outdoor environment, Outdoor Classroom programs emphasize supporting children as independent learners, bringing what was indoors outdoors, and cooperating with other teachers. You must address such issues as site and climate conditions, the yard's natural features, the general layout of activity areas, appropriate equipment, and maintenance of natural and human-made features.

Reflection

Review your teaching staff, program design, and environment. For each, rank in order of importance the three greatest strengths and three greatest opportunities for improvement. Sit down with some or all of the center's staff and ask them to do the same. Post the responses and talk with each other about the elements you see that can support the Outdoor Classroom.

CHAPTER 3

Getting Buy-In from Stakeholders

ADULTS ARE THE MOST IMPORTANT FACTOR in a successful Outdoor Classroom. Although the program is designed for children, it's the product of a collaboration among adults. Teachers, of course, are critical to its function, working with children, activities, and environment. Administrators and managers provide funds and approve of the program. Parents enroll their children. Designers make sure the outdoor spaces work best for the program's goals; decisions by other adults help shape the spaces. Members of society at large must support the concept in their roles as regulators, legislators, and advocates.

Understanding the Stakeholders

Let's take a look at how each of these groups becomes a player in establishing the Outdoor Classroom.

Teachers

Teachers are the most important adult players in the Outdoor Classroom. You can make the Outdoor Classroom happen, even when others are unsupportive or in opposition. The action of a single teacher can make the difference. It's not uncommon for a lone teacher to nurture elements of the Outdoor Classroom by establishing a garden, initiating outdoor games, or implementing content, such as art or music, outdoors.

A single teacher cannot create an Outdoor Classroom that serves a full center. It takes a substantial part of the teaching staff as a whole to do so. Obviously, the more the better. Realistically, as in all aspects of early childhood education (ECE) programs, individual teachers offer different strengths, interests, and orientations. For the Outdoor Classroom to function well, two teacher-related conditions must be in place. First, the administration must establish the Outdoor Classroom as a policy for the center. This means, at a minimum, that all teachers will cooperate with the program. Second, a sufficient number of staff must be willing to implement it. That number will differ from site to site, and it needn't be a majority. What's important is that each classroom has a teacher who is committed to implementing the Outdoor Classroom and a large enough number of teachers in the program to keep it going.

This group is responsible for creating, developing, and maintaining the Outdoor Classroom. The group must be able to work together effectively, articulate the goals of the Outdoor Classroom to others, and garner the respect and support of less interested teachers.

Administrators/Managers/Owners

While teachers are needed to turn the Outdoor Classroom into a reality, they can't do it without the blessing and support of administrators,

managers, and/or owners of the center. These individuals control the money and have veto power over what happens at the location. In many cases, the center director can become the spark plug that drives the Outdoor Classroom. The director can also act as benefactor, making sure the program has adequate financial support while leaving its implementation to the teachers. The director may also block implementation entirely by refusing to allow it.

Those who serve on governing boards also have critical roles to play. To the degree that they are involved in daily operations, they can help supply funding for the Outdoor Classroom or block its implementation.

To play their role wisely, administrators need to understand the overall goals of the Outdoor Classroom. If they are going to be the program's driving force, they need to understand it well enough so teachers will be motivated to act. In most cases, it's the other way around: staff educate administrators about the Outdoor Classroom. Depending on where the initial interest lies, teachers and administrators will educate each other.

Parents

Parents are important partners in the Outdoor Classroom. Enthusiastic parents often help to develop the play yard, contribute materials, and even help with some of the activities or lessons. Sometimes parents have serious concerns and may question the effectiveness of an outdoor program. It is important for those of you who are staff members to equip yourselves to explain the benefits of the program and to address any concerns parents may have about their children being outdoors so much of the time.

Ideally, an early childhood program will promote itself as having an Outdoor Classroom. Experience has shown that when parents compare programs with and without the Outdoor Classroom, the former benefits from increases in enrollment. Nonetheless, teachers and administrators still need to continually educate parents, telling them about Outdoor Classroom activities and helping them appreciate their children's outdoor experience.

Parents who understand and appreciate the Outdoor Classroom may contribute to its expansion in their children's ECE and elementary school experiences. Their understanding and participation should be encouraged.

Designers and Others Who Produce High-Quality Outdoor Environments

A high-quality Outdoor Classroom can't exist without a high-quality outdoor environment. Responsibility for the outdoor physical environment is in the hands of a large number of people. These include ECE teachers and administrators, maintenance staff, program owners, governing boards, landscape and building architects, playground designers, vendors of playground equipment, and construction personnel, including specialists in landscape grading, plumbing, electrical, concrete, carpentry, gardening, equipment, installation, and general contracting.

Getting all of these individuals on the same page may seem nearly impossible. Many of them have little in common. They may not know each other or even be involved with the play yard. But if the yard is to be truly successful for children and teachers, all of these individuals need to work cooperatively. Anyone from these specialties can have a negative impact on the play yard for generations of children and teachers.

This pool of people needs to understand two things: first, the design of the play yard must benefit children. It is not being built for the ease, glory, or profit of adults. Second, everyone involved needs to be mindful of well-defined objectives and guidelines for the design of quality play yards.

While it would be nice if all of the participants were knowledgeable and committed to what is best for children, ultimately the ECE professionals must provide the guiding perspective. To do so, they must be able to articulate the necessary concepts of an Outdoor Classroom play yard, drawing on their understanding of design, construction, and maintenance of spaces that work developmentally for children and that support the program. Early childhood education professionals should supply other members of the team with the following information:

- concise descriptions of the Outdoor Classroom
- explanations of its importance
- reasons for addressing common concerns of others in the group
- ideas on design and construction
- examples of other Outdoor Classroom environments
- other professional resources

Appearances can be deceiving; this classically misdesigned yard has at least twenty-three design errors because qualified ECE-based design input was not obtained (see appendix E).

While ECE professionals must take leadership roles in a yard's design, they must also recognize the value of what each of the other participants brings to the table. The ECE professionals should take the lead in providing content and facilitating conversations. They must model the behavior they want to see. Other members of this large group will come to conversations about the play yard with their own agendas. If they are presented with clear, coherent, and comprehensive information to guide their contributions, the results are much more likely to benefit children.

Society at Large

Beyond the individuals directly involved in creating an Outdoor Classroom lies a much larger community. To a significant extent, current ECE outdoor programs, especially their environments, are products of these communities. People commonly think about large bodies as beyond their control, but individuals make individual decisions and take individual actions. When we look at community this way, we can see more opportunities to change things, beginning with the way we ourselves do them. Up to this point in time, the creation of outdoor play spaces, and the programs that populate them, have been greatly influenced by the elements of this larger community. It includes the equipment manufacturing industry, architects, regulators, legislators, layers of administrators who have to approved play yard construction projects, contractors, and members of boards of trustees.

Development, production, and marketing of products have profound impacts on play yards. View any number of play yards, and the unfortunate pattern of placing the play structure in the middle of the yard becomes obvious. This is no accident. It represents a confluence of marketing, selling, and choices made by ECE professionals and the vendors of playground equipment. Once it becomes a norm, it is adopted by the people who make decisions on purchases and placement of equipment but who lack ECE training. Thus poor processes can perpetuate themselves.

Once established, such norms become difficult but not impossible to change. Change occurs when individuals decide to do things differently.

Evaluating Staff Readiness

No matter who starts to develop the Outdoor Classroom, teachers must ultimately embrace it if it is to be successful. To address staff effectively, first consider the staff as a whole, not only in regard to the Outdoor Classroom. You may need to fundamentally alter the condition of the staff as a whole. If staff are usually positive, you may need to do little. If they are not, you'll need to do more. One index of staff contentment is their willingness to work together and share supervisory responsibilities for children in the play yard who are not from their own rooms. Getting teachers to share responsibilities outdoors may be best addressed by changing their attitude about working together and sharing responsibility. Developing the Outdoor Classroom may require changes within the culture of a center at the deepest level.

Condition of the Staff

The term *condition of the staff* refers to performance, behavior, attitudes, skills, state of mind, and well-being. It is reflected in the idea of job satisfaction, but it also includes perceptions of managers' satisfaction with staff's performance. Staff cannot be truly satisfied in their jobs if their supervisors are unhappy and vice versa.

Over thirty years ago, when my wife, Elyssa, and I were first planning our center, we made what may have been our most important decision. It arose from a simple idea: "If the teachers are happy, then the children will be happy. If the children are happy, then their parents will be happy." We realized that the key to our success lay with teachers; their well-being needed to be always at the top of our agenda. Our program has a strong core of long-tenured staff at every level and a community of teachers, parents, and alums who continue to remain remarkably well connected over three decades. Our dream of creating a high-quality educational community and program has been realized well beyond our initial vision.

Certain elements of the center's culture related to staff are particularly helpful in developing the Outdoor Classroom:

- enthusiasm for continuing program improvement

- willingness to work together on something new

- commitment to doing what is best for children

- appreciation of the outdoors

- skill in developing and working from a vision-led model of education

Staff Development for the Outdoor Classroom

The focus of staff development for the Outdoor Classroom includes three major topics:

1. Creating a positive orientation

2. Creating a safe working environment by fostering a culture of caring, learning, and personal responsibility

3. Learning to communicate

Developing these three topics creates a culture in which the Outdoor Classroom can thrive. They address teachers' attitudes, skills, and behaviors. Every ECE center develops these elements to some degree. Achieving certain standards of behavior in each of these areas is necessary for the Outdoor Classroom to be effectively implemented.

Creating a Positive Orientation

Arguably, the most important trait for staff to demonstrate in the culture of a center is a positive attitude. The quality of experience for children and everyone else rises or falls on this quality. While a center's positive culture may frequently be the result of leadership that is personality driven, positive orientation can also be learned and taught. A positive culture can be created. It requires strong leadership and at least some staff who know how to build it.

Fostering a Culture of Caring, Learning, and Responsibility

Some people can be positive under any circumstances, but for most of us, learning how to be consistently positive requires a safe environment. Just as we don't purposefully raise children in negative environments, so we should not subject adults to emotionally unsafe ones. Businesses often go to great lengths to ensure employees' physical safety, but creating psychological safety is not as easily or as frequently attempted. A psychologically safe environment empowers employees to be more articulate and assertive. This demands more strength and skill from supervisors. Such an environment only works in a business model that sees all participants as equal partners with different roles.

The responsibility for creating a safe working environment resides solely with the supervisor or director, who sets the tone for the program at that site. Tone is the *feeling* of the place. In a workplace, setting the tone can mean many things. Often it is tied to workplace behavior and performance in the production of a product, as well as to how supervisors and staff behave toward one another. It may even include how staff members are expected to dress.

Because of the pressures on ECE programs to prepare children for kindergarten these days, the tone in many programs has become one of "kindergarten prep." Supervisors expect teachers to push children to perform to a fixed set of standards. The objectives of the program are based on preparing children for an imagined future performance rather than on the present. This is not the focus of the Outdoor Classroom. Our early childhood work is built on relationships, so the tone we set must address how we work with the children.

Ideally, the staff of a child care center or preschool functions like a healthy family: the adult relationships serve as models for the children. Just as important, the staff members must be supported in ways that reinforce the skills they need to use in working with the children.

What do the guidelines for a psychologically safe working and learning environment look like? Three basic guidelines apply to the well-being of both children and adults:

1. Don't hurt yourself and don't hurt others.

2. Take care of yourself so you can take care of others.

3. Use everything for your personal improvement, learning, and growth.

These guidelines reflect a learning orientation to life, one that views relationships as the primary vehicle through which human beings learn and mature. Thus one reason for focusing on safe environments is to support staff in their own learning and growth. In a real sense, the learning environment for children and the learning environment for teachers are the same. Operationally, they should function seamlessly.

An educational model in which teachers are expected to learn and grow with the children is very different from the traditional model, in which the teacher knows all and the children know little. To a certain degree, the philosophy of the Outdoor Classroom turns the traditional notion of education on its head. Children are capable of leading their own learning, and teachers must remain active students. Teachers who never stop being students approach the children they work with differently. The Outdoor Classroom intends for teachers to demonstrate a high degree of sensitivity to children, reflecting a keen, sensitive, open, and nonjudgmental view of the outdoors and their own learning process. In the Outdoor Classroom, who you are determines how you function as a teacher and how you relate to the children.

The qualities, skills, behaviors, and understanding that are required to create and maintain a positive center culture are common to both adults and children.

Life is for learning. The events of our lives are our curriculum. Everything that happens in our lives is for us. Nothing is really against us. It is all *for* our learning and growth. We can expect that our lives will present us with things that challenge us. We have all the resources needed to deal with them.

External experience mirrors inner reality. There is an intimate relationship between what goes on around us and what goes on inside us. Surrounding events and environments provide us with opportunities for learning and growth. They should not be blamed but should be used for our learning.

Mistakes are a natural part of learning. In the long term, failure is a temporary condition. Everyone is capable of learning. Mistakes are part of the learning process. A mistake does not make someone bad or stupid.

We are all responsible beings. We are capable of learning how to work effectively with our thoughts and feelings so they don't run us. Taking responsibility for how we handle things empowers us and gives us freedom.

We need to be compassionate. Learning and practicing compassion for ourselves and others is a critical part of the learning process and forms the foundation of successful learners, teaching us how to deal appropriately with mistakes and how to work harmoniously with others.

These ideas describe the positive culture that best supports the Outdoor Classroom. It is a culture that sets expectations of staff, particularly in their relationships with others, and focuses on personal responsibility. There is no space for blaming someone or something else. Everyone is on an equal footing because, whatever his or her job title, everyone is learning. Expectations are both firm and reasonable. Staff members are responsible for their actions but are not blamed for mistakes. They are encouraged to treat others the same way and to work together to problem solve rather than to point fingers. Everyone is accountable. Everyone is expected to support everyone else.

Learning to Communicate More Effectively

In an ECE setting, communication underlies everything that happens, especially relationships, which are the foundation of all ECE work. Whether it is intentional or not, every ECE program is a relationship-based one. The entire focus of ECE work rides on relationships. Relationship-based curriculums are not unique; all curriculums are delivered through relationships, and the delivery vehicles are themselves curricula.

Communication skills are not usually taught as part of core ECE curriculum, certainly not at the two-year college level. Centers that want to foster strong relationship-based programs need to carefully examine the communication skills of their staff and the standards they set for communicating.

Staff may or may not have thought about the value of communication training. It may be necessary to have some conversations about why this is important. You can pose the question, "Have you ever been negatively affected by a miscommunication or the way in which someone communicated to you?" A survey is one good way to do this, because people may be more likely to share their real concerns if they can remain anonymous. They may find it illuminating to play the childhood game Telephone, in which individuals quickly listen to and then repeat a sentence to the next person in a circle, then discover how much the sentence has changed during many quick transfers of information. Usually, after some discussion, staff acknowledge the need for improved communication.

Communication skills are taught in many ways. There are dozens of skills that can be learned. These are fundamental:

- **Being present.** The most important communication skill is not really a skill. It's how you feel inside yourself while you are with another person. Most people are preoccupied with something other than being present to the person with whom they are communicating.

- **Heartfelt listening.** Heartfelt listening means that you listen with your ears, your eyes, your mind, and your heart. You are listening not only to someone else's words but also to that person's emotions.

- **Asking open-ended questions.** Open-ended questions invite the person to say more than a simple yes or no. They open the possibility for any response.

- **Perception checking.** Although we may be present and listening in a heartfelt way, we may not always understand what the other person is expressing. When you check your perceptions, you share what you think someone else is saying to check if you are correct.

Engaging the Staff: Allocating Responsibility for Implementation

Staff can be organized to implement the Outdoor Classroom successfully in a variety of ways. At least one staff person in a center must become the main leader. This person will help maintain focus on organizing and implementing the project.

Usually the person initially interested in promoting the Outdoor Classroom is one teacher or the director of a center. Often she has attended a workshop or conference on outdoor learning and brought back the information to her program, hoping she can infuse others with her own enthusiasm. Spreading her enthusiasm to the staff makes undertaking the project much easier. Leadership can be divided among teams or groups; it can come from the teaching staff rather than being driven by the director.

Examples of Staff Implementation

Implementation requires leaders and staff. Here are descriptions of ways that successful projects have formed.

Assistant director and forty staff. An assistant director at a faith-based center singlehandedly brought the idea of establishing an Outdoor Classroom program to her director and staff. Initially, only a few staff members showed interest. The assistant director worked steadily over a period of two years, getting groups of teachers to attend workshops and visit other Outdoor Classroom sites. Eventually all of the staff members became enthusiastically involved.

Director and specialist teacher with twenty staff. A director partnered with a part-time teacher who was interested in outdoor education. Initially about half the staff came on board, but it took about a year of small steps, including visits to other Outdoor Classroom sites, before the entire staff became enthusiastic participants.

Director and assistant director with sixty staff. In this large program, the director partnered with her assistant director. The staff were

housed in two locations and starkly divided in their opinion of the Outdoor Classroom, depending on the location where they worked. Benefiting from the leadership of the assistant director, the staff at the larger location came on board fairly quickly after attending a conference and visiting an Outdoor Classroom site. They focused on learning enough about the Outdoor Classroom to communicate its value to parents so activities like mud play would be accepted by them. The teachers at the larger site received an award of recognition for their project, and this helped bring staff at the other location into the fold slowly over the following year.

Committee of teachers with sixteen staff. After six months of on-site training and consultation, the director of this workplace-based center found staff evenly divided in interest. With one group of teachers determined to move forward, the director allowed this group to organize as the Outdoor Classroom committee and take charge of implementing the program. This group accepted the challenge and assigned the other teachers to outdoor activities. They also taught the second group how to teach the Outdoor Classroom's activities.

Director and twelve staff. The director of a Head Start program found herself at a new site, a 1930s elementary school with a grassy playground that needed to be converted into a preschool play yard. Virtually all of her teachers were very skeptical about going outdoors and allowing the children to play with loose parts such as milk crates. After attending a workshop and visiting an Outdoor Classroom site, the teachers reluctantly tried the crates and some other loose materials. After just a few days of watching the children play, the teachers began enthusiastically developing the yard further, establishing garden boxes, dramatic play, and many tabletop activities.

Teacher leading the director and fifteen staff. The renovation of an all-asphalt ECE site in a very large school district began with the efforts of one teacher to establish a large garden. Working with the permission of his director, he singlehandedly got the project started and engaged families and other teachers with his ideas. Their efforts were rewarded when the program was granted $300,000 by the district to overhaul the play yard.

Director and all staff together. In this small, private, for-profit center, where the staff were very close-knit, enthusiasm was instantaneous after the director took the staff to training. The director asked for a letter from the Outdoor Classroom Project documenting the center's participation in the project so she could share the letter with the families. The result was a family workday that transformed the yard and set the stage for the program to become a demonstration site.

In each of these cases, some member of the group had received enough training to take the lead in starting an Outdoor Classroom program. Getting others engaged, however, usually took visits to other sites combined with additional information about the Outdoor Classroom; this was usually obtained through workshops or training at the center.

Summary

A broad group of stakeholders must come together collaboratively and cooperatively for the Outdoor Classroom to be implemented successfully. This group includes teachers, administrators/managers, parents, designers, others involved with facilities, and society as a whole. Of this group, teachers have the greatest impact on the quality of the Outdoor Classroom. The conditions, needs, and concerns of staff must be understood as part of winning their support for the Outdoor Classroom. Staff development should focus on creating positive attitudes, a safe working environment, and a culture of caring, learning, personal responsibility, and effective communication. There are a variety of ways to organize staff to implement the Outdoor Classroom.

Reflection

Reflect on your stakeholder groups. Besides your teachers, are there any other groups you need to work with to make your Outdoor Classroom possible? List three areas of professional development that you think can help your staff with this process. How will you implement staff development in these areas? What will be the best way to organize staff to implement the Outdoor Classroom?

*Badly deteriorated spaces can languish for years due to lack
of interest or obstruction to change grounded in lack of understanding
of the importance of quality outdoor spaces.*

CHAPTER 4

Getting Started

IMPLEMENTING THE OUTDOOR CLASSROOM may require staff to make some changes in their thinking about teaching and children. For most people, change does not come easily. Happily, because of their underlying philosophy and principles, Outdoor Classroom projects create enthusiastic responses in many people: staff, children, and families. This chapter offers a general approach to cultivating and creating the changes needed to implement the Outdoor Classroom.

As an early childhood educator, your business is to foster change. Yet many teachers are challenged when asked to change how they do things. Teachers' resistance to working outside is the biggest impediment to getting children outdoors. Resistance to changing the philosophy and practices of facilities and maintenance departments also inhibits the improvement of play yards. Resistance to changing funding priorities inhibits governing boards and administrators from providing financial support for implementing the Outdoor Classroom.

Opening People's Hearts and Minds to Change

People open themselves to change differently. Some respond to reason, others to emotion, and still others to what they can actually see. There is no one correct approach. One way to encourage change is to identify something that needs changing and explain why. Another is to offer an example of the change where it has already been successfully accomplished. Simple enthusiasm about change can be contagious and can encourage others. Because what motivates people varies, use as many approaches as possible to garner the widest support. Visit sites where the Outdoor Classroom has been successfully established—this has proved to be the single most powerful method of encouraging change. All of these approaches have generated significant success.

Immediate Small Steps

To be most successful and avoid pitfalls, you need to plan thoroughly for change. At the same time, beginning the process of change as quickly as possible is beneficial. Initiating small changes can break through the status quo and create momentum for change. Success breeds success. Immediate small steps require little planning, no approval by others, and little or no money, and they can be implemented right away. One example is increasing the amount of time children spend outdoors. Another is taking an activity outdoors for the first time, such as reading to the children. A third is teaching children the names of all the trees in the yard. Experience shows that when small steps are taken, larger steps frequently follow.

Short-Term Tactics

Short-term strategies can be accomplished within a few months. They should specify specific outcomes. These strategies require planning and possible expenditures of money and/or time and materials. An example is rebuilding and expanding a sandbox. Another is adjusting staffing so teachers can work more effectively together, encouraging several classrooms to share the yard at the same time, and then implementing the plan. A third is conducting a meeting with families to explain the value of the outdoor activities that teachers are planning. Short-term strategies go smoothly when all of the involved adults agree on them. Such strategies can be useful in implementing one or more elements of an Outdoor Classroom as part of a long-term strategy or when a long-term strategy is being developed slowly.

Long-Term Strategies

Long-term strategies involve specific elements or comprehensive implementation of the Outdoor Classroom. Specific elements can be as simple as saving money for an expensive piece of equipment or saving for its installation. Another element may be planning and renovating a section of the play yard. Comprehensive implementation may involve all of a center's outdoor environment and all aspects of its outdoor program. A long-term strategy for comprehensive implementation is commonly designed and carried out over several years, allowing for steady progress while taking into consideration other elements like fundraising and staff development.

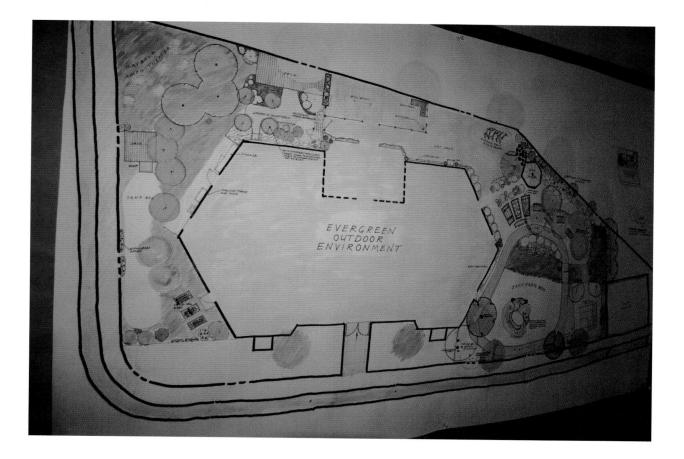

Your Role in Facilitating Change and Implementing the Outdoor Classroom

Initiating the Outdoor Classroom obviously requires the efforts of many people. Even when it is initiated by an administrator, teachers must ultimately adopt leading roles. For those of you who want to embark on such a mission, here are a few things to consider.

The Roles of a Change Agent

If you are an early childhood educator and you want to implement an Outdoor Classroom, you are a change agent—a facilitator of change. Others involved in implementing the Outdoor Classroom, such as architects or contractors, are change agents as well, though in a narrower sense. Early childhood education (ECE) teachers and administrators take on making the broadest range of changes, even when they don't have other formal leadership responsibilities inside your organization. Your responsibilities may include a number of roles:

- **Anchoring.** The educator serves as the person in the organization whom others recognize as maintaining institutional focus on the Outdoor Classroom.

- **Evaluating, initiating, and creating.** The educator looks for ways to implement the Outdoor Classroom by creating new environmental and program elements.

- **Leading.** The educator takes a leadership position within the staff team and is willing to lead others in developing the Outdoor Classroom.

- **Modeling.** The educator walks the talk and models the behavior she wants other staff members to emulate.

- **Articulating.** The educator communicates with others in the language of the Outdoor Classroom, sharing its philosophy, principles, and practices. This is done in informal, workday conversations, formal presentations, and written documents.

- **Mentoring and training.** The educator coaches and trains others so they can help design and implement the Outdoor Classroom.

Maintaining a Positive Attitude

A consistently positive attitude is required of anyone who wants to encourage others to develop an Outdoor Classroom. Positive energy usually draws other people in. Optimism touches and stimulates what is positive in others. It is not coercive. It is inspiring. It stimulates and energizes people.

Maintaining a positive attitude is affected by the center's existing culture and philosophy of working with children. How are new ideas treated? As with any change, the culture of a center is put to the test. As an agent of change, you may find yourself needing to do more than you anticipated. Some changes in the center's culture may be required.

Not every staff member is going to feel the same about the Outdoor Classroom. Some may wish it had never come up. Others can hardly wait to get started. It's important that everyone respect one another's feelings.

If you're not sure how to proceed, consider these questions:

- What happens to centers where new ideas aren't given a chance?
- Do teachers and children thrive in those programs?
- What kinds of behavior extinguish a child's enthusiasm for learning?
- What dampened *your* enthusiasm as a child?
- What kinds of behavior tend to create enthusiasm?
- How important is enthusiasm to children's learning?

Enthusiasm is essential. And that's one of the great strengths of the Outdoor Classroom: it generates enthusiasm.

Three Barriers to Change and How to Overcome Them

To be successful in cultivating the change needed to implement the Outdoor Classroom, you need to understand common barriers to change and how to overcome them.

Inertia, enthusiasm, vision, and "yes." A common barrier to change is inertia—the resistance of things to alter their energy state. It takes energy to overcome inertia. This can be frustrating for people because it's hard to tell in advance how much energy will be needed. People often give up before change has begun to occur. While inertia is often clothed in policies, rules, and regulations, in the end, it is sustained by people. It's the inertia of people's attitudes and behaviors that you must overcome first. What most frequently extinguishes enthusiasm is someone who says immediately, "We can't do that because . . ." You know people often feel that saying yes is a big commitment, so your best response when you sense reluctance to a new suggestion may be to say, "Let's look at that!" Most people are willing to look as long as they don't feel they have to buy.

Enthusiasm and vision can overcome inertia. It's Martin Luther King Jr. saying, "I have a dream." It's a teacher saying, "I have an idea." It's a child saying, "Let's play!" Then it's someone saying, "Yes!" Or it may simply be someone who doesn't say no.

The unknown, courage, and persistence. Change is always a step into the unknown. Making change requires courage and persistence. Think of the American Revolution, the fight for freedom from British rule by the masses led by Gandhi, or the crusade by farmworkers' for their rights led by Cesar Chavez. Neither the participants nor the leaders knew the outcome; they only knew they were on a path they believed in. People with courage have intimate relationships with truth. No matter what truth shows up, they're going to treat it as the next step in their process of discovery. When Thomas Edison was trying to invent the lightbulb, he failed hundreds of times, but he used each experiment as a lesson in what not to try again.

When we approach the unknown that way, we do not experience failure—just new information that tells us to try something else next time. People like Edison, Chavez, Gandhi, King, and those who worked tirelessly with them treated the unknown as if whatever they learned from it was something of value. They believed that unless they moved forward into the unknown, they would never learn everything they needed to help themselves and the people they cared about. They persisted because they were not willing to live lives in which people missed opportunities because they were reluctant to move forward.

The already known and creative, positive thinking. Perhaps the most common barrier to change is what people are *sure* they know. If only just a few others, who are convinced they are right, disagree with them, the zeal of those advocating for change is often drained away and their effort for change is slowed, if not stopped. One of the best ways to counter this inertia is to describe a similar situation with a different outcome. Better yet, show people one if you can. Knowing something else is possible helps people open their thinking to changes. Thinking outside the box may accomplish the same goal. Creative thinking respects people's current beliefs and still poses the question, "Could there be anything more?" This encourages people to explore further. It's important to help others realize that many other possibilities exist.

The Outdoor Classroom's Development Plan

Effective, long-term, permanent change can be broken down into a series of steps that answer these questions:

1. Where are we?

2. Where do we want to go?

3. What should be our initial changes?

4. How do we get there?

5. How do we actually do it?

6. How do we know when we have succeeded?

7. What if we have challenges?

8. Who needs to be acknowledged?

Centers become involved with the Outdoor Classroom in a variety of ways. They begin with their own version of the Outdoor Classroom at different degrees of development. Some may treat their outdoor time and environment just as a recess from being indoors. Centers with a modest level of development may utilize the outdoors for a longer period of time, but may not have the outdoors or the outdoor program very well organized, so children just "run around." A few centers may have fairly developed Outdoor Classrooms but not be able to articulate them as such. Wherever the developmental starting point, progress can be made. A single staff member may attend a workshop or conference or read this book and become committed to the program, but for the entire center to successfully implement its own Outdoor Classroom, other staff members need to join that one person at the start of the journey.

How you and your colleagues enter the process greatly affects your likelihood of success. In working with hundreds of centers and thousands of teachers, I have found that the more that adults reflect on and share their own early childhood outdoor experiences, the more enthusiastic they become about the program. Depending on how you begin your involvement, you can accomplish what's needed in several ways. If you are presenting information at a staff meeting, use a relatively brief activity at the start of the meeting—for example, pair participants, give them an assignment, and then ask several of them to share their results with the group as a whole. If you are getting together to talk about the *possibility* of starting the Outdoor Classroom, you may need longer conversations to cultivate others' interest in the concept.

Step 1: Where Are We? Evaluation, Information, Discussion

During this first step, you examine what is already there in your program and develop an understanding of the Outdoor Classroom. Staff members are introduced to the concept by observing and evaluating the existing "Outdoor Classroom" in which they work (the outdoor environment, the curricular program provided outdoors, and teacher practices outdoors), reading about the Outdoor Classroom, and having discussions to help them understand one another's perceptions and interests. If the staff is not already a cohesive team, you should work toward creating such teamwork. The ease with which commitment to the Outdoor Classroom occurs largely depends on the extent of staff cohesiveness. Step 1 involves learning about the Outdoor Classroom through group discussions. Ideally, prior to or along with evaluation of the quality and completeness of a center's existing outdoor program, practices, and environment, staff members obtain information about the Outdoor Classroom program. Having a basic understanding of its philosophy, principles, and practices helps you with evaluation. You may want to provide your colleagues with written information. Reading this book is one option. Others include the following:

- **Conferences.** Many ECE conferences offer sessions on outdoor learning. These may offer detailed introductions to the philosophy, principles, and practices of the Outdoor Classroom. Some conferences center around themes, such as outdoor learning or learning in nature.

- **Workshops.** Less complete and detailed than conferences and usually more narrow in scope, workshops can provide specialized understanding about outdoor learning.

- **On-site training.** Specialists in the field of outdoor learning, or specifically the Outdoor Classroom, provide on-site staff training. Such training, consisting of one or more events, may focus specifically on evaluation and discussion.

- **Site visits.** Staff members can visit other programs that have implemented the Outdoor Classroom. These visits provide direct examples of what others are trying to accomplish and allow staff members to talk with people who have been through the process.

- **Staff-led discussions.** Depending on the individuals and the training they have received, you may be able to lead one or more informational discussions for staff members.

At some point, you'll find it's time for a serious conversation among staff members. This needs to be a true conversation and not simply an edict that comes from the director. Unless everyone participates and feels he or she is part of the process, effective implementation of the Outdoor Classroom will be difficult.

The conversation will be unique to each center. The primary objective is for staff to determine exactly where they are and then to come to a consensus that moves them to the next step.

Step 2: Where Do We Want to Go?
Setting Priorities and Defining Outcomes

At some point, the discussion comes to a point at which it makes sense to start planning for changes. This is a critical juncture, a time when the evaluation you've undertaken will either be richly used or, in extreme cases, bypassed and replaced with actions that are not well thought out.

Any changes made in one area of an ECE program are likely to affect other elements of the program. This is certainly true of the Outdoor Classroom, which usually demands changes in the physical environment, the program, and the staff. For example, addition of a water play element may require more supervision by staff. Increasing the amount of time children spend outdoors may require more coordination among staff from different classrooms.

The Ideal Scene

Using the concept of the Ideal Scene in your planning helps to ensure that all aspects of the Outdoor Classroom will be considered, alone and in relationship to each other. Designed to be a collaborative process with staff, the Ideal Scene can also make use of input solicited from parents and children, thereby helping to build community and positive interpersonal relations.

It's been said that action follows thought. The Ideal Scene is a representation of your thoughts. In this case, it's your vision of the Outdoor Classroom. Creating an Ideal Scene is like painting a picture, using words instead of paint. An Ideal Scene is a complete description of a situation or experience you hope to achieve. It may contain a variety of goals. For example, you may want to make children healthier. You may want to make children more successful learners. Both of these goals could be part of your Outdoor Classroom's Ideal Scene.

The Ideal Scene is composed of a set of statements that describe what you want to achieve. These statements are made in response to questions like: What would it look like? How would it feel? How would it work? Who would be involved? What would its characteristics be? The answers to these questions comprise your Ideal Scene. Here are some guidelines to help you write your Ideal Scene statements effectively.

- **Present-tense statements.** The statements should be written in the present tense, as if what they describe is happening right now. Writing in present tense brings your vision into the present. Avoid words such as *wish, want,* and *like,* because they keep your vision hypothetical. Consider the difference between these statements: *I want to buy a car* and *I am buying a car.*

- **Clear and measurable statements.** Statements should be written so that it's easy to assess when you've accomplished them. Consider the difference between these two statements: *I'm buying a car someday* and *I'm buying a Mercedes Benz SLK300 next Tuesday.* The second statement is clear and measurable. The first is not, because it contains no data that can be used to determine your progress toward your goal or to determine if it has been accomplished.

- **Positive statements.** It often feels easier to express things negatively than positively. This doesn't work with Ideal Scene statements, which should be positive. Negative statements like *I don't like my car* don't move toward positive outcomes. Negatives may need to be acknowledged, but they can be stated in positive ways—for example, *I'm replacing my worn-out car with a new one.*

- **Statements without limits.** Never place limits on your Ideal Scene. Always leave room for new possibilities. State the minimum you hope for, and remain open-ended about the maximum: *Our children are enjoying a minimum of an hour more per day outside.*

- **Statements that are 50 percent believable.** Ideal Scene statements need to be achievable. They also need to exceed the limits we are used to accepting. Using this guideline can reveal significant differences in what staff members think is possible. This is one place where the consensus may need to be worked at a little, encouraging those who are more skeptical to allow a little idealism or hopefulness to creep into their thinking.

Following are some examples of how to write statements for Ideal Scenes:

The teachers are really enjoying reading stories to the children outside under the oak tree every day.

We have plenty of outside storage, so taking out and putting back equipment is really easy.

The children enjoy riding their trikes on our new trike path.

The children are spending at least three hours per day outside.

Here are some examples of how *not* to write statements for Ideal Scenes:

We'd like the teachers to read stories every day. *(Not in present tense)*

We don't want to have to carry stuff outside. *(Vague, negative)*

The children need trikes. *(Not measurable; future oriented)*

The children spend exactly three hours per day outside. *(Places a limit)*

The $5 million grant from United Way is helping us create a perfect play yard. *(Unrealistic)*

Some additional guidelines that can help you create an Ideal Scene:

- **Completeness.** The Ideal Scene needs to be complete. Don't leave out anything that is important or necessary to the other parts of the Ideal Scene. For example, if you're going to have a sandbox, don't forget the water! If your center is in the desert, don't forget the shade!

- **Harmony.** The elements of your Ideal Scene should be harmonious. Don't include items that are mutually exclusive. For example, "The children ride their trikes anywhere in the yard" is not consistent with "There are lots of quiet places for children to enjoy relaxed activities."

- **Images, not action steps.** Sometimes Ideal Scene statements are confused with action steps. Remember: Ideal Scenes are powerful images of what you want to achieve, not lists of action steps. For example,

Ideal Scene: "I am joyfully playing and having fun when I exercise."

Action Step: "I am exercising three times a week, 30 minutes at a time."

Ideal Scene: "I am appreciating the beautiful flowers and lush plants that surround my home."

Action Step: "I am planting two trees and seven kinds of flowers outside my house."

As you create your Ideal Scene, you may want to organize your thinking about the following:

- children's experiences
- curriculum
- teachers' experiences

- physical environment
- staffing
- indoor-outdoor flow

As a group, list all of your ideas. Once they're listed, organize them; group similar ideas together. Consensus should be reached on how to organize items as well as on what to include and what to leave out in the final listing. The final product should be a picture of what the staff collectively wants its Outdoor Classroom to be when it becomes fully implemented. This discussion may take several meetings to accomplish. The important thing is that consensus be achieved.

Setting Priorities

Ideally, priorities are set after the Ideal Scene has been completed. You may need to prioritize during the grouping or categorizing parts of your discussions. For example, you may have funding that needs to be spent by a certain date or legal/regulatory pressure to correct something in your outdoor environment. These can't wait.

You can employ a wide variety of criteria for setting priorities—for example, immediate needs, safety or regulatory imperatives, personal desires, perceived value to children, marketing or public relations value, interests of parents or families, children's interests. Individuals may develop their priorities based on different ways of valuing these criteria, but the priorities of teaching staff and administrators usually offer the most useful perspectives for making these decisions.

One important consideration is how easy or difficult it will be to accomplish a goal. Successful implementation of the Outdoor Classroom relies on establishing and sustaining momentum, particularly when there's a lot to be done. Starting with priorities that are easy to accomplish builds a sense of achievement that encourages continual involvement and progress.

Equally important is the sequence in which steps must happen. For example, for activities to be set up outdoors, you may need to prepare outdoor areas so they have nearby storage. Money may need to be raised to purchase new equipment for the outdoor space.

One way to start setting priorities is to ask each staff member to review the Ideal Scene and identify her own top priorities. This can be done so anonymity is maintained. Once individual priorities have been recorded, they can be tabulated and the group's overall priorities determined. Again, the group may want to discuss priorities and reach a new consensus.

While center staff are working on the Ideal Scene and establishing the group's priorities, everyone needs to come to an understanding of consensus. Consensus does not mean that you agree with everyone about everything; it means that you can live with a decision. Consensus that merely achieves "I can live with it" for a large percentage of the staff should not be the goal. Most staff should be enthusiastic supporters; only a few individuals should have to live with it.

Defining Outcomes

The purpose of the Outdoor Classroom is to improve outcomes for children. A by-product should be improving outcomes for staff and parents. All of the Ideal Scene elements need to be connected to specific outcomes.

Outcomes are overarching goals with smaller objectives built into them. They should be measurable and clear so you can assess whether they've been achieved. It may help you to think of outcomes holistically: how they fit together into a greater whole. For example, one overarching ECE goal or outcome is literacy. Letter recognition is one small objective along that path. Another outcome is providing physically challenging outdoor environments. One of several objectives building toward that outcome might be installing a new section of trike path with some hills, curves, and bridges as part of it.

An example of a possible outcome for children could be "to develop a better understanding of nature." Sample elements or objectives for this outcome might include these:

- being able to identify three trees by name.

- knowing through hands-on experiences that many plants come from seeds.

- being able to explain why rain is a good thing.

- understanding that plants make it possible for us to breathe.

Examples of possible outcomes for teachers include the following:

- understanding the relationship between children's experiences and learning opportunities

- developing more meaningful relationships with children

- advocating for outdoor play

- dressing for active play with children

Possible outcomes for designing the environment might include these:

- challenging children physically

- including textural elements

- meeting the physical and observation needs of teachers

Remember that the Ideal Scene can always change as new information becomes available. It's not set in stone; instead, it serves as the goal toward which staff now move. (See appendix F.)

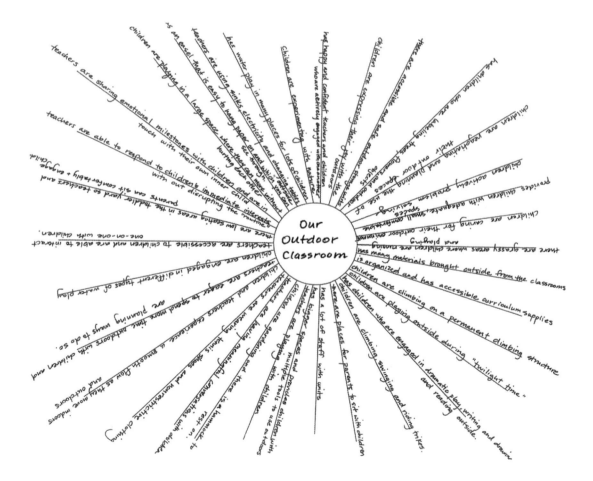

Step 3: What Should Be Our Initial Changes? Optional Interlude

Initial exposure to the Outdoor Classroom frequently energizes participants to want to take immediate action. This can be both positive and negative. Taking small, immediate steps at first can demonstrate the positive benefits of the program and inspire others to action. It can also have the opposite effect by causing some colleagues to become resistant or antagonistic to change.

Change is safest when it is begun after the full staff have become involved and have agreed on how to move forward. That said, change is possible at any point and can be achieved when the following guidelines are adhered to.

Small Changes Work Best

In the beginning, small changes are best because they're easier to accomplish. They are also less likely to generate negative reactions. Teachers who can't wait to begin making changes must trust that starting out small holds the greatest potential for long-term success.

Do Things You Can Maintain

Building steady momentum is important for everyone involved. Establishing a high-quality, high-functioning Outdoor Classroom is a process, not a single event; it's a distance run, not a sprint. You build it through dozens of small actions assembled over an extended period of time. One of the reasons for doing small things first is that they are easier to maintain than larger initiatives. For example, beginning a gardening project with a single small planter box or a set of small pots is far easier than cultivating a large garden plot. It's important that once you get started, the activity is not dropped but steadily maintained as a permanent part of the curriculum.

Rock the Boat Gently

While the size of the initial change is important, so is its impact. Even a small change can be disruptive if it differs markedly from previous practices. For example, a teacher decides that the children in her care can go barefoot when she knows that other teachers don't allow their children to do the same. Or perhaps she permits her children to have water play on a cold day, and this practice has not previously been allowed. Teachers who initiate new activities on their own should be sensitive to established practices and aware of other teachers' sensitivities.

This isn't to say that many changes can't be made smoothly and peacefully. Here are a few examples:

- **Placing flowers and plants in pots and planters outside.** Following attendance at an Outdoor Classroom conference, one teacher purchased two pots of flowers and placed them on either side of the door to her classroom. It was a simple and inexpensive act, yet as parents came into her classroom, all of them noticed. Their questions ranged from "What's the occasion?" to "Did someone die?" to "Is it someone's birthday?" Each time she was asked, the teacher had an opportunity to share her excitement about what she had learned at the conference with the families. By the end of the day, she had a group of interested and informed families.

- **Spending more time outdoors.** It may seem obvious, but simply increasing the amount of time children spend outdoors can be a significant step toward realizing the Outdoor Classroom. It requires only the decision to do it. Of course, doing so has further implications for staffing, curriculum, and yard development. But if more outdoor time is introduced gradually, an extended program can be developed.

- **Playing with children more when they are outdoors.** This may be a simple step to strengthen teachers' connection to the children, especially if teachers have had a pattern of standing back as monitors. It may also encourage teachers to support children in their outdoor activities.

- **Moving indoor activities outside.** This can be simply done with items that are easy to move back and forth and that will hold up well outdoors. An outdoor lunch or circle time might be a good place to start. Some programs even have naptime outdoors.

- **Opening classroom doors, creating indoor-outdoor flow.** This is another simple act, but one that requires a plan for staffing. Creating the opportunity for indoor-outdoor flow can greatly improve children's behavior by giving more active children more opportunities to be outdoors.

- **Organizing and cleaning out storage areas.** This activity can help the program and creates no demands for additional work beyond the initial organizing and cleaning.

- **Speaking with families informally about the benefits of outdoor play.** This is another activity that can have a positive impact without creating new demands. It can encourage families to support more outdoor play at home.

- **Allowing children outside in the rain.** It may seem surprising, but teachers have been motivated to use this as an initial activity with great success. Of course, it requires planning and a strong relationship with children's families.

Step 4: How Do We Get There? Creating an Action Plan

While it's possible to take many small, unplanned actions in support of developing your Outdoor Classroom program, a center is much more likely to be successful when staff members take time to plan comprehensively. The Ideal Scene process, including setting priorities and reviewing outcomes, establishes a firm foundation for planning. Successfully translating the elements of the Ideal Scene into a harmonious and vibrant Outdoor Classroom requires organization. This approach is called an *action plan*.

To those who are inexperienced in using an action plan, doing so may seem like an unnecessary burden. However, the rapid pace and fragmented nature of daily life in child care makes a structured approach to getting things done necessary. This is particularly true when you are implementing large-scale projects. Organizing an approach to change increases the likelihood of success. Not organizing almost ensures difficulty or failure in achieving your objectives. Many worthy ECE projects fail just because effective approaches weren't used.

Using a Simple Action Plan Structure

The structure of an action plan is simple and easy to understand. Anyone can use it effectively by following these steps.

1. **Identify the objective.** Look at the objectives that were developed as part of the Ideal Scene when you established your priorities. Confirm their alignment with desired outcomes. Select one objective or a related set of objectives to act on.

2. **Describe action steps and set a schedule.** Identify the steps needed to reach the objective. Set an activity schedule and assign a date for completion.

3. **Identify the person(s) responsible.** Assign responsibilities to specific individuals for implementing each step and monitoring progress.

4. **Implement the actions.** Carry out the action steps.

5. **Track progress and acknowledge success.** Establish a schedule of meetings to track progress, address emerging issues, and acknowledge efforts.

Creating and Implementing a Successful Action Plan

While the Action Plan process is simple, several elements are key to success:

Small, achievable objectives. Limit the items you select to small and achievable ones—this is the most effective way to build your Outdoor Classroom. Success is easier with small, simple tasks than with large, complex ones. It is more encouraging to attempt and rapidly achieve a number of small objectives than to spend a lot of time trying to achieve a large one. Building a pattern of successful implementation through small sequential successes strengthens the ability of participants to get things done.

Clearly and completely defined objectives. The more clearly and completely an objective is defined, the easier it is to achieve. Unclear objectives make it difficult to identify specific action steps.

Measurable objectives. Part of defining an objective is making it measurable—that is, describing it in a way that lets you know when you have achieved it. For example, you could define construction of a trike path as complete when all of the concrete has been poured. Or completion could be defined in other ways—for example, when landscaping has been added around the path or the trike storage shed has been built. Any of these choices would constitute a valid definition of *measurable*. The specific measurable description just needs to be spelled out.

Sequenced objectives. Considering that you may want to pursue many objectives while you're developing your Outdoor Classroom, you need to organize them in the way that makes them easiest to accomplish by identifying how they relate to each other. This includes sequencing them in appropriate order so the preconditions for successfully accomplishing a task are always completed before you start the next phase. For example, you may need to relocate a climbing structure to make room for a new tire swing. Relocating the climber will require you to determine where you can put it or, perhaps, decide simply to remove it altogether. So, the sequence of activities would be to locate a space for the swing, measure it to be sure the swing will fit, determine a new space for the structure to be moved, measure it to be sure it will fit. Then you can order the swing, move the structure, and install the swing. You may also need to organize a series of small, unrelated objectives according to other priorities in the development of your task list.

Clear and complete task list. The task list is your description of everything that needs to be done to accomplish your objective. Those responsible for achieving it need this list to guide them. Others need it to evaluate whether the activity is on target.

Let's look at an example of how this process works, beginning with the Ideal Scene statement.

Ideal Scene Statement:
The children are happily riding their trikes on the one-way trike path that runs around the perimeter of our yard.

Objective:
Completion of a concrete trike path 42 inches wide and 3 inches thick that runs around the perimeter of the preschool yard, a distance of about 300 linear feet.

Task List:
1. Meet with staff to determine best location for path; identify any obstructions that may need to be removed.
2. Produce scale map with a precise drawing of location of path and items to be moved or removed.
3. Secure parent volunteer team to remove obstructions; set up Saturday workday.
4. Secure three bids for installation of path by contractor; select contractor; set up date for installation.
5. Coordinate parents' workday.
6. Monitor contractor's installation of path.
7. Hold grand opening of trike path.

Assigned responsibilities. One person, acting alone or with others, is ultimately responsible for whatever is accomplished. Identifying who is responsible for each step of a project is necessary to ensure that it gets done. One person should be specifically assigned the responsibility for completing each item on the task list. This is not the same thing as demanding that this person do it alone. As you can see from the example above, most of the tasks require a group of people. The person who is assigned responsibility is charged to stay on top of the task to ensure that it is completed. That could mean doing it alone, doing it with others, or monitoring others while they complete the task.

At least one person needs to monitor the individuals who are assigned to each task.

Reasonable schedule. Establishing a timeline for accomplishing the project and its individual tasks is the only way to ensure the project's completion. The schedule allows those responsible to monitor the progress of project work, prod workers if necessary, and evaluate the results of work completed.

Regular meetings. Many well-intentioned projects fail because progress is not adequately managed. Holding regular meetings to track progress is critical to the project's success. Meetings should be scheduled regularly, well publicized, and open to anyone who's interested. This helps to ensure ongoing, broad-based support. Challenges commonly arise during projects, and regular meetings provide opportunities to address them. By bringing problems forward in a group setting, team members are relieved of the burden of addressing them alone. The wisdom of the group can be applied to finding solutions. Regular meetings also provide opportunities to support and acknowledge people who are working on the project.

Planning Leaders

For the planning process to work, one or more people must lead. While planning for the Outdoor Classroom requires the entire team's participation, not everyone needs to be involved all the time or assume the same roles. A group of people can lead the planning process. These planning leaders are responsible for doing the following:

- setting up and running planning meetings

- making sure that information generated at meetings is recorded

- supporting the planning process until an action plan has been created

Some groups may want to rotate leadership. This works when a number of people possess strong leadership skills. When a team has consistent, quality leadership, they will be more likely to achieve their goals.

The Importance of Including the Entire Staff

Members of the group who are not leaders often think they have minor roles. This isn't true of center staff, all of whom are involved with the action plan, directly or indirectly. Neither the group nor the process can work without them. Each staff member helps with the planning work by attending meetings, contributing ideas, coming to consensus, taking minutes, or conducting research between meetings. Possibly the most important role staff play is supporting movement toward goals. Usually this means listening, supporting, and encouraging others; sharing; and being willing to come to consensus.

Holding Meetings to Create the Action Steps

The action steps needed to achieve your Ideal Scene will be unique to your center. Depending on how many objectives you pursue at once, developing action plans may require one meeting or a series where specific goals and objectives are identified and prioritized and action steps are organized sequentially.

Creating an Outdoor Classroom Committee or Task Group

Because developing the Outdoor Classroom involves more than action plans, it's helpful to have a permanent committee. In many cases, centers establish an Outdoor Classroom Committee before starting the development process so an ongoing group can shepherd the project as it evolves. If such a committee has not been established by the time your staff starts its action planning, this is a good time to form it.

Step 5: How Do We Actually Do It? Implementation

Implementation is included in the action plan but is also a separate step with its own requirements and potential pitfalls. Your ECE personnel need to understand it.

Ways of Approaching Implementation

The evaluation, Ideal Scene, and action plan prepare a center to implement an element or elements of the Outdoor Classroom. Depending on the task, implementation can be accomplished by staff, other professionals, or volunteers.

Obviously, it's possible to implement elements of the program without evaluating, visioning, or planning. This may happen in some programs, depending on the extent to which these centers already have

A complex, crowded yard like this requires a thorough evaluation of the environment and a clear overall design plan before making changes if costly mistakes from piecemeal yard improvements are to be avoided.

Outdoor Classrooms. After being formally introduced to the Outdoor Classroom, staff of centers with well-developed programs may feel that they can bypass step-by-step development and simply make changes based on the new information they've received. Strangely enough, staff of centers with minimally developed programs may do the same, perhaps because they're overwhelmed by the prospect of embarking on step-by-step changes. For still other reasons, some centers may choose to bypass one or more of the formal steps and go directly to implementation, whatever the program's stage of development.

Before making any of these choices, your center should fully weigh the value of completing the evaluation and the Ideal Scene. Many of the problems I've seen in existing outdoor programs and environments are the result of insufficient thoughtful evaluation or planning. Completing the evaluation can help make your changes as beneficial as possible.

The Ideal Scene is designed to help you capture the full range of what you envision and to identify your priorities. You aren't obligated to implement all of them immediately, or even to implement them at all. Implementing elements you have identified in your Ideal Scene will increase the likelihood of their benefiting the program and the children

because they have been thoughtfully developed as part of a cohesive whole. Elements not in the plan can be implemented as well, but there is a greater likelihood that their implementation will have unintended consequences, because the impact of their presence in the Outdoor Classroom has not been thoroughly considered. This is particularly true of small installations, such as a marimba placed in concrete footings without consideration of long-term needs for the space in which it was located. A year later, staff may want to use the space for something else, and the marimba will have to be uninstalled.

Staff may want to look at how other sites have implemented elements similar to the ones you are planning.

It's common to use paid professionals and nonprofessional volunteers to help you develop your Outdoor Classroom, particularly when you're working on the outdoor environment. Remember that you're responsible for meeting all applicable regulations regarding anything that you might have them construct. Consultation with a licensing evaluator, playground safety inspector, or landscape architect may be required to ensure compliance with state and federal regulations. Not adhering to such regulations, whether or not they are required by your specific governmental agencies, can expose you to lawsuits should anything go wrong.

Step 6: How Do We Know When We Have Succeeded? Monitoring, Tracking, and Evaluating

Monitoring means keeping in touch with everything that happens during implementation. Tracking is comparing what is happening against the schedule to see if elements are being completed on time. Evaluation is assessing what needs to change, based on what is happening. These activities should be assigned to one or more individuals and discussed at each monitoring meeting. Maintaining a checklist of items to be monitored along with the schedule is very helpful.

Step 7: What If We Have Challenges? Course Corrections, Plan Changes, and Adjustments

This step is rarely considered, yet is almost always needed. Projects seldom go exactly as planned. Step 7 addresses this reality. If your team finds that implementation is not progressing as planned, you need to consider adjustments.

Effectively Making Course Corrections

Recognizing that something is not working is seldom a happy discovery. What's important, though, is not that something isn't working but how you handle that discovery. The most important action to avoid is finger-pointing: assigning or casting blame shouldn't follow from assigning responsibility. Blame seldom, if ever, moves a project in a positive direction. This is why I use the term *course correction* when I talk about addressing challenges.

The first task is to make sure that the challenge or difficulty has been accurately identified. The solution to a misidentified problem usually doesn't work very well. A good strategy is to ask for suggestions from those closest to the problem. They are usually the most knowledgeable, and they can exercise their responsibility by offering suggestions. Whatever remedy they propose, use the group to validate it. Encourage everyone to think outside the box. As Einstein said, "A new type of thinking is essential if mankind is to survive and move toward higher levels" (*New York Times*, May 25, 1946). Consider all the options. Don't be afraid to be brave. Usually the group has the answer.

Step 8: Who Needs to Be Acknowledged? Giving Credit Where Credit Is Due

Unfortunately, this step is often forgotten or otherwise doesn't happen often enough. Acknowledging people's efforts communicates the value of their participation. By doing so, you fuel people's enthusiasm for continuing their involvement and making their contributions. Always include all members, even if you only acknowledge them as members of the group. Acknowledge not only success but also the qualities that have

made success possible, such as effort, persistence, consistency, courage, cooperation, support, thoughtfulness, and critical thinking.
You really can't give enough acknowledgment.

Summary

Developing your Outdoor Classroom involves change. Change can be accomplished by taking immediate, small steps and by using short- or long-term strategies. Change requires a change agent—someone who can initiate and guide the change process. Using an Outdoor Classroom Development Plan or some of its elements can help your center become more effective in implementing the program.

Reflection

On a scale of 1 to 5, with 1 being most ready, identify how ready your center is for change. If you identify yours at 3, 4, or 5, you may need to do some additional work before starting to implement the program. If your center is ready for change, review the eight steps of the Development Plan. What makes the most sense to start with? Create a plan for your center, and be sure to consider all the steps.

A thorough outdoor yard and program evaluation directed the removal of this structure, doubling the open, grassy area available for running and field games while still leaving a full-size climbing structure farther back for children.

CHAPTER 5

Evaluating the Outdoor Classroom

EVALUATION IS CRITICAL to developing an Outdoor Classroom. It's only through evaluating what you have that you can identify the actions you need to take. Developing the Outdoor Classroom without first evaluating your program's needs is like building a house without a plan or performing surgery without knowing what needs to be fixed or removed. Deciding to make changes is always based on some level of evaluation, even when it's only a fleeting perception followed by a quick judgment. If you want to make significant, successful, long-term change—before, during, and after implementing the Outdoor Classroom—then you need to undertake thorough evaluations.

What Is Evaluation?

Evaluation begins with observation. For the purposes of the Outdoor Classroom, observation can be defined as observing all of the outdoor elements of an early childhood education (ECE) program in order to understand them better. Once you've accomplished this, you can make changes that you consider valuable to children's development. Evaluation is performed with a measurement instrument or by comparing your program to a set of standards. In ECE, we evaluate programs for a variety of reasons:

- to measure children's development
- to measure the effectiveness of a program, a curricular approach, or an activity

- to measure children's use of space or activities
- to measure children's patterns of movement through an environment
- to measure effectiveness of staff development or parents' education
- to measure parents' satisfaction

The Evaluation Process

All evaluations require gathering information or data. Observation is a common element in gathering information for ECE programs. There are dozens of ways to record observations, including writing them down, capturing them with audio and video technology, and collecting artifacts like items from children's portfolios. As you embark on the data gathering process, it is important to be aware of how your own attitudes and biases about the children, childhood, or children's behavior might influence how you gather data. You, like every other person, see life through the *perceptual filter* of your own unique experience, understanding, and values. For instance, some teachers don't like to take notes, others are uncomfortable with cameras, and some don't value children's artwork as much as other teachers. Because we all have biases, it is helpful to work as a team in gathering data, respecting others' viewpoints, and sharing data obtained in different ways. This strategy will create the richest and most inclusive pool of information on which to base your evaluations.

Examples of Evaluation Instruments

The field of ECE has been dominated by several evaluation and standards instruments. These include the Early Childhood Environmental Rating Scale (ECERS) and its related instruments and the accreditation standards produced by the National Association for the Education of Young Children (NAEYC). Considering their overall size, neither of these instruments focuses much attention on the outdoors. In fact, until recently, few instruments have evaluated the outdoors at all.

More recently, the Preschool Outdoor Environment Measurement Scale (POEMS) was developed at North Carolina State University by a multidisciplinary team led by Karen DeBoard (Child Development) and Robin Moore (Landscape Architecture). On its website, www.poemsnc .org, POEMS is recommended for these uses:

- A checklist for childcare teachers/caregivers and administrators interested in learning more about creating higher-quality environments for children's outdoor play and learning.

- A checklist for directors and program administrators planning quality outdoor environments for young children or those who are working to improve their existing space.

- A reference tool for landscape architects and designers working with childcare programs to design quality outdoor play and learning spaces.

- A guideline for new construction of child care facilities.

- A reference tool for funding agencies supporting healthy, high-quality outdoor play and learning environments for children.

- A source of guidance for policy initiatives in early childhood development.

- A research instrument to study the implications of outdoor environmental quality on children's development and learning.

The Outdoor Classroom Staff Perception Survey

The Outdoor Classroom Staff Perception Survey was developed specifically to facilitate evaluation of ECE outdoor programs interested in implementing the Outdoor Classroom. The survey covers these topics:

- outdoor environments
- activities
- teachers' practices
- teachers' and administrators' attitudes
- children's behavior

Since 2003, this survey has been used by hundreds of centers. It has assisted them in evaluations that guide their development of Outdoor Classrooms. The evaluations aid program development rather than teacher or child performance. The survey has also been used to measure progress in implementing the Outdoor Classroom. It was created to provide a foundation for the development of the Outdoor Classroom as described in this book. The survey's objectives are these:

- inspire and guide your center in developing and implementing its action plan

- provide a baseline measurement of the extent to which selected elements of the Outdoor Classroom are already established in your center

- identify the degree to which your center is prepared to develop the Outdoor Classroom and what issues should be addressed to move forward

- measure progress over time in developing selected elements of the Outdoor Classroom

The survey can be used by all teaching and administrative staff who are regularly involved in the program. It's fundamentally a reflection or perception assessment—that is, it asks you to reflect on your experience, past observations, and current thinking about the condition of your program. It measures staff perception of the program and does not ask you to directly observe and record program conditions.

The shared perceptions that result from this kind of survey are meant to prompt discussions among staff. These, in turn, are intended to encourage teamwork, so the Outdoor Classroom can be implemented and teachers can agree on the best strategies for doing so. Validating perceptions through this instrument also goes a long way toward validating teachers.

I recommend that groups discuss results after they first complete the survey. Doing so fosters greater accuracy because individuals can clarify their perceptions in conversation with each other.

Any evaluation tool, the Perception Survey included, provides only a snapshot of your center. The survey can be completed in twenty minutes or fewer. In some cases, data from the survey may point to the need for more information or additional work with staff to clarify the results.

Distributing and taking the survey. I recommend that all staff complete the survey at the same time, preferably during a staff meeting. The survey is intended for those of you who work directly with children in the classroom as well as program directors. Results are more reliable when staff members do not discuss how to respond but instead rely on their own perceptions.

Confidentiality. Depending on the culture of your own center, you may believe that confidentiality of individual survey results is important. The staff as a whole should determine if you want surveys to be confidential.

When privacy is important, staff should be able to return surveys anonymously.

Using the survey results. Survey results form the basis for initial discussions among staff about your outdoor program. From there, an action plan can be developed to design and implement your own Outdoor Classroom. Survey data form a baseline against which data from later surveys can be measured. Using the action plan, you can look at the variations between the earlier and later surveys to see if progress is being made.

Sample Survey Questions

More than any other factor, adult attitudes determine whether the Outdoor Classroom can be successfully implemented. Teachers, administrators, and parents control children's access to the outdoors and the quality of their experience there. No matter how rich the outdoor environment or how skilled the teaching staff, if adults are not motivated to support and implement the program, the Outdoor Classroom won't happen. Conversely, if teachers in your program are enthusiastic about getting children outdoors, implementation can be successful even with less than great outdoor space and teachers whose skills are not optimal.

The responses to questions on the Perception Survey are organized on a six-point scale:

1. Strongly Disagree
2. Disagree
3. Somewhat Disagree/Agree
4. Agree
5. Strongly Agree
6. Don't Know

This scale measures progress—or lack of it—over time and provides your teachers with a range of responses so they aren't placed in the forced-response position of saying yes or no to questions where more shaded responses are possible. The survey includes statements like this for participants to respond to:

- I'm enthusiastic about getting the children outside.
- My co-teachers are enthusiastic about getting the children outside.

These statements evaluate the current state of affairs and help to identify the staff attitudes that need to be worked on. An average overall score of 3 suggests that staff need little or no additional work to motivate them to become involved in the Outdoor Classroom. A score below 3 suggests that work needs to be done with the staff before you begin developing a program.

The next set of statements considers the attitudes of the adult groups that might influence the implementation of the Outdoor Classroom.

- Among our teaching staff, there is enthusiasm to further develop our outdoor program.
- Our teachers are open to change and new ideas concerning our curriculum.
- Our director supports further development of our outdoor program.
- Our parents support further development of our outdoor program.
- Our owner or board or administration above our director supports further development of our outdoor program.

These statements identify the work that needs to be done to generate support among adults to implement the Outdoor Classroom. For example, some adults may express the belief that the center is just fine as it is, without further development.

Evaluating the Outdoor Classroom Program

Program is the second of the three key elements comprising the Outdoor Classroom, along with staff and environment. Program includes these elements:

- children's pattern of being outdoors
- how outdoor activities relate to indoor activities
- activities in which children engage
- how activities are organized
- philosophy of working with children and practices of teaching

Children's pattern of being outdoors. Children's pattern of being outdoors is the most important element to look at in evaluating an Outdoor Classroom program. Nothing happens without the children. Two critical factors must be considered:

1. the length of time children spend outdoors

2. how frequently children go outdoors

How outdoor activities relate to indoor activities. Here is a simple question you and your staff should ask yourselves: How many activities that you currently undertake indoors can children engage in outdoors? For the Outdoor Classroom to be complete, the answer should be "all." Unless a full range of outdoor activities are available, some children prefer to remain inside because of activities that are uniquely available there. One objective of the Outdoor Classroom is to encourage children who are less inclined to be outdoors to spend more time there. Children who want to be outdoors more of the time need the opportunity to participate in a full range of activities outside so their development can be balanced. Indoor and outdoor environments need to become a level playing field.

How activities are organized. The placement and organization of activities have a significant impact on their effectiveness. Each activity should have its own designated space. To avoid conflicts, activities shouldn't overlap each other. In some cases, activities benefit from being placed alongside each other. Organization includes having sufficient, convenient, and appropriate storage space for activities. For example, sand storage should be located in or next to the sandbox, and the storage box should be large enough to accommodate adequate supplies.

Philosophy of working with children. Appropriate and effective organization of activities is based on the conviction that children are active learners. Otherwise, what gets replicated is the same teacher-driven environment that too frequently characterizes indoor environments. The outdoors should offer a much more dynamic range and depth of activities for children. If teachers' expectations of children remain the same outdoors as indoors, little has been accomplished by moving activities outside. Teachers who require quiet voices and neatness inside need to drop those requirements when children move outside.

Many practices should be reconsidered when you move activities outdoors. Perhaps the most common one is where control lies: it should be turned over outdoors to the children. When it comes to activities, you should consider the play yard as a blank canvas that offers children access to any materials they want to work with and allows them free rein to use those materials. The only limitation should be that they don't hurt themselves, each other, or the environment.

Allowing children to take the lead in developing their activities places you in a supporting, rather than a directing, role. It encourages you to focus on observing and understanding the children, and leads to a much more child-centered approach to teaching. Observing and understanding are key to identifying the unique learning style of each child. When children have more control over their activities, they learn responsibility, problem solving, communication, and social skills at levels that can't be achieved through teacher-directed learning.

Evaluating the Play Yard

When your objective is to implement the Outdoor Classroom, evaluating the play yard becomes a complex challenge. There's no tradition of subjecting play yards to careful scrutiny, largely because in the past they weren't considered part of the learning environment. Considering the amount of time that children spend in educational facilities today, it's odd that most ECE environments are remarkably uninspiring and disconnected from designs that could support learning, like natural spaces and indoor settings with abundant daylight and access to the outdoors.

In ECE, evaluation of outdoor space, program, and staff should be seen as an interrelated whole. This is particularly important in evaluating outdoor space. The environment influences the quality of activities and teachers' practices, but alone it cannot create an Outdoor Classroom. For example, skilled teachers and portable activities can create an effective Outdoor Classroom in a yard offering nothing but grass. But the best environment imaginable cannot ensure a successful Outdoor Classroom without skilled teachers and a solid program.

Effective evaluation of outdoor space requires a broad understanding of outdoor spaces and how they function in a child care setting. Evaluating the yard can be broken down into three facets: (1) health and safety, (2) aesthetics, and (3) utility.

The quality of most play yards in American ECE programs ranges from inadequate to wholly unacceptable by the standards of the Outdoor Classroom. With tens of thousands of play yards in operation, ECE programs can only hope to bring most of them up to an acceptable standard over time. The first order of business is to recognize and acknowledge the yards' current limitations. These spaces were never conceived as learning environments equivalent to indoor classrooms. They were intended as places for recess and letting off steam before children went back inside, where the real learning would take place. This means that even in those few cases where spaces have been designed with intention, their intentions work against optimal use for the Outdoor

Classroom—for example, the climbing structure in the middle of a yard, surrounded by poured-in-place rubber. Such a place can never be central to children's outdoor activity and learning.

Entrenched misdesigns mean that to move in the direction of environments suitable to the Outdoor Classroom, substantial parts of the yard must be altered. Frequently this means removing hardscape and relocating equipment. Because of the cost and difficulty of demolition, the magnitude of the task of relocating equipment can bring change to a halt. Although evaluation may call for change, developing an Outdoor Classroom–friendly space often is most effective when staff initially work *around* permanent structures in the yard.

Ensuring the Safety of Children

A second, more complex impediment to improving play yards is resistance to change masked as health or safety concerns. Of course, protecting the health and safety of children is necessary in all ECE settings. That's not the impediment—the impediment is making safety the *purpose* of environmental design. If protection were the principal reason to work in ECE, you would expose children to nothing, since everything has an element of risk. Early childhood education would not be about the development of children—it would only be about their absolute protection from risk.

The Outdoor Classroom is grounded in the conviction that children must act to learn—not simply listen to adults. Children need to take on challenges and risks so they can master what they need to know. Mastery can only be achieved by confronting challenges, risking failure, and developing patterns of success through repeated efforts, punctuated by moments of learning through the results of their actions.

To ensure safety in the implementation of the Outdoor Classroom, adults must keep at the forefront of all that they do that our goal and mission is the development of children into capable and competent adults. Think about the outdoor environment as a purpose-driven place for learning, one in which safety is *a* consideration but not *the* raison d'être. For example, it's unlikely that you'd suggest that an activity area of an indoor classroom, such as the blocks area, be eliminated because something hazardous could occur there, like a child throwing a block.

Yet outdoor activities—swinging, sand play, and building with sticks and branches—are often banned by adults because someone has perceived them as a health or safety problem.

The traditional approach to health and safety is to prevent danger *to* children. While this is obviously important, it's not an educational approach. It doesn't teach children anything because it doesn't allow them to get close enough to danger to understand and master it. It actually makes children less safe, because when adults aren't around, the children have no experience in handling the dangers they've been protected from.

The Outdoor Classroom's approach to ensuring children's health and well-being is to teach them to *learn* how to be healthy and safe. Learning requires doing. Rather than thinking about how much to keep children away from, you focus instead on how much you can support children *to do.* The Outdoor Classroom is designed to challenge, provoke, encourage, and support children in ways that are developmentally consistent with their capabilities.

Evaluating and Preparing the Outdoor Environment

As you go forward, you'll discover that very few child care sites have harmonious relationships with their outdoor environments. This is unfortunate. Children deserve the best places possible. Psychologically, they internalize what their surroundings teach them: the environment is one of their teachers. They learn through their interactions with it. Activities outdoors could not occur in the same way indoors. Despite the limitations found in most yards, because of the importance of outdoor environments, it is imperative that we find an effective way to improve them.

Looking at basic yard layout. A center's play yard is connected to and impacted by the environment surrounding it. The points of connection are where the edges of the yard touch the exterior spaces. These touch points are called *interfaces*. Each of these interfaces affects how the yard functions and how it influences the health and well-being of the children, the yard's aesthetics, and the utility of the space. For example, it makes a difference if the property bordering a play yard is a junkyard, a street, or a beautiful park. The play yard also has a shape defined by its perimeter, and this creates one or more geometric spaces within which activities occur. Evaluating the impact of spatial relationships and forms is critical to the evaluation process.

Interfaces with other yards can be turned into visual barriers while serving as an activity area, like this fence garden.

Before a play yard fills with activity areas, equipment, and children, it's just space, like that of an empty indoor classroom. Unlike an indoor classroom, however, whose size and footprint have been specifically designed for ECE purposes, the play yard is almost always space defined merely by the adjacent building's outline and what's left over once the building has been constructed or acquired. Ideally, property for a child care center would be purchased with a particular center–play yard configuration in mind so both building and yard could be built as a seamless whole; indoor and outdoor spaces could be treated as a single classroom. This is almost never the case. If you're working with an existing center, almost by definition you are working with space that's less than ideal.

This alleyway (20 feet wide by 200 feet long) was considered acceptable outdoor play space for a new downtown center after appropriate space was suddenly withdrawn from the project.

To effectively implement an Outdoor Classroom and improve an existing play yard, you must first evaluate the yard's basic layout and understand its spatial relationships and interfaces. These elements define what you can do with the yard you have. Your evaluation should imagine the basic yard without its current uses, existing equipment, and developed surfaces, such as concrete and grass. As long as you envision the space with its existing structures in place, you're depriving yourself of possible alternatives, some of which are probably much better than what you already have. Although the yard's basic layout limits what you can do, it can also help you develop it.

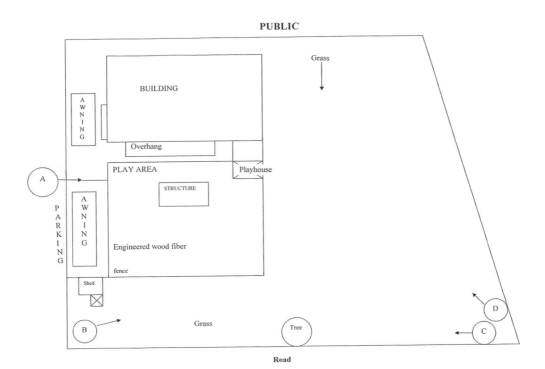

View from (A) (see above).

View from (C) (see above).

Size. No matter how the yard is laid out, you'll find that size is always the prime consideration. The bigger the yard, the more you can do with it. While teachers may worry that larger yards are inherently more dangerous because they are harder to supervise, smaller yards are probably in fact more dangerous. Smaller yards provide fewer choices for children in a more crowded space, so adults must direct children's activities more intensely and closely. Smaller yards can become so crowded with equipment that you have difficulty supervising children well.

Child care center yards are often unnecessarily kept small because officials lack a fundamental understanding of the needs of young children.

Size also influences how space can be used and the number and kind of activities that can be carried out in it. Smaller yards preclude some activities and equipment, such as swings, open space, and trikes.

Size affects the yard's aesthetics in several ways. Lack of space means there's little room for decorative plantings, although even small yards can be designed attractively. Cramped yards may affect children's sense of opportunity and enthusiasm, diminishing their eagerness for taking initiative and being creative.

Because this small space was assigned to infants, it was carefully designed and landscaped with edible plants. It now works beautifully for the purpose intended.

Form and spatial relationships. Form and spatial relationships define how the different spaces in the yard are structured and related to each other. In the simplest situation, where the yard is close to square or rectangular in shape and lacks irregular features, not much consideration is usually given to these elements. As shapes become more extreme or irregular, form plays a more significant role. For example, a rectangular yard that is thirty feet wide and ninety feet deep has a spatial dynamic that' very different from one that is ninety feet wide

and thirty feet deep, if only because its area extends sixty feet farther from the building than that of the wider and shallower yard. Multiple yards—usually created to separate children of different ages from each other, as specified by government regulations—have internal and external spatial relationships. External relationships are usually limited to their interfaces. For example, no interface exists between an infant yard and a preschool yard if they don't touch. Philosophically, a program may prefer that younger and older children not share a common fence. Or a program may choose to have the play spaces of these age groups share a common border so the children can communicate with each other.

Health and safety issues related to spatial relationships mostly involve adult supervision. Ideally, all locations in a yard should be visible from any other location. In practice, even in square yards, ill-considered placement of equipment or plantings can block your sight lines. An irregularly shaped yard may actually *improve* your ability to supervise, depending on the shape of the space and the placement of equipment and plantings.

Yard form and spatial relationships profoundly influence the Outdoor Classroom. Evaluate your yard by imagining the ways activities could be distributed and come up with ways to lay out spatial relationships so they benefit children and teachers.

Think about the aesthetics of your yard when you evaluate yard form and spatial relationships. Unfortunately, the yards of most child care centers are not attractively laid out. Use odd forms or spatial relationships to create beauty.

The common placement of climbing structures in the middle of the yard impedes supervision.

Well-designed yards make use of every inch of space to add interest and beauty.

Spaces that can be hidden from view, such as the sides of buildings, need to be fenced off or gated.

Composition and content. Up to this point, my discussion of evaluation has asked you to consider the play yard as a blank canvas on which you paint details and then an Outdoor Classroom. Only after you have done so should you look at the composition and content of the yard. It's too easy to walk directly into a yard and immediately become distracted by its internal features—that is, mistaking the forest for the trees. In fact, the composition and content of the play yard rely on and are influenced by other elements. An activity area or piece of equipment can work differently in different contexts. For example, a structure equipped with a south-facing slide works very differently when it is shaded by a neighboring tree than when it stands alone in open sunlight. Where you place a sandbox has everything to do with how much use it gets.

As an evaluator, you must consider health and safety, utility, and aesthetics while you review the following elements:

1. **Adjacency.** Play yards should always be adjacent to the classrooms of the children they serve.

2. **Space.** Play yards should always be large enough to contain the full variety of activities children need for healthy outdoor development.

3. **Layout.** Open space (usually best positioned in the center of the yard) should be large enough for children to run freely; activity areas should be placed around the yard's perimeter.

4. **Separation.** Yard layouts should separate children's activities that might conflict when they overlap. Separating them reduces risks and challenges to supervision.

5. **Completeness.** Healthy outdoor development occurs only when there is a full range of activities that address the whole child.

6. **Materials/equipment.** A wide variety of materials and equipment are needed, particularly items that children can manipulate.

7. **Storage.** Adequate outdoor storage must support the full range of children's activities.

8. **Challenge.** Play yards should provide challenges sufficient to support development of the whole child; "challenges" here means "reasonable risks."

9. **Nature.** Nature and a natural environment should be the dominant environment outdoors, in contrast to the cement, asphalt, rubber, and metal that characterize many play yards.

10. **Philosophy.** Quality Outdoor Classrooms require more than a well-designed play yard; to be effectively implemented, the program philosophy must mandate and support appropriate activities and teacher practices.

Substituting open lawn for a climbing structure in the middle of the yard creates both a more natural and more usable central yard space.

Summary

Evaluation is essential to the creation of an Outdoor Classroom.
A variety of evaluation instruments are available, and one, the Outdoor
Classroom Staff Perception Survey, has been specifically designed to support the creation and development of an effective Outdoor Classroom.
The Perception Survey looks at three areas: (1) what children do,
(2) what adults do, and (3) characteristics of the program.

   Most play yards have significant shortcomings that require thorough
assessment and remodeling. Safety in design is critical, but is not the
purpose of design. Yard design should focus on developmental benefits
for children.

Reflection

How well do you know your outdoor environment, program, and practices? How do you currently evaluate them? If staff were to do a full
evaluation, do you think their evaluations would be similar or different?
What do you think are the most important elements in need of change
in the three areas of program, teacher practices, and environment?

CHAPTER 6

Program and Implementation Strategies

BY LAW, every early childhood education (ECE) program must have an outdoor component, so each offers, at least in a rudimentary sense, some elements of an outdoor program. But a true Outdoor Classroom, as I've described it in this book, must possess a particular bundle of components. It should do the following:

- consider indoor-outdoor flow of children

- increase outdoor time for children

- help teachers learn to relinquish control

- support children's engagement

- consider desired outcomes

- establish activity centers

- support child-created activities

In this chapter, we will look at strategies for implementing each of these elements.

Considering Indoor-Outdoor Flow

Plans for indoor-outdoor flow help children move seamlessly back and forth between the indoors and the outdoors. When the play yard is adjacent to the classroom, you may be able simply to open the door and encourage children to spend more time outdoors. Combining indoor and outdoor spaces offers a number of benefits.

- **Increased space.** By connecting the two areas, you greatly increase the amount of space available for children to play in. More space can reduce conflicts that arise from crowding.

- **Greater selection of activities.** More activities can be available at one time; their variety can be broader. Activities that children can't do indoors become possible outdoors.

- **Accommodation for a wider range of behaviors.** Increasing the amount of time children spend outside helps those who need to be more physically active but are constrained by indoor regulations, need more space, or need a more nature-based setting.

- **Expanding the ways children can learn.** Making the outdoors readily available supports active learners whose learning style, even for tabletop activities, require them to be more physically active.

- **Improving children's health.** Giving children opportunities to spend more time outdoors increases the likelihood that physical activity will become a regular part of their day and that they will adopt more active lifestyles as permanent behavioral patterns.

Saying yes to opening the door to the play yard is the first step in implementing the Outdoor Classroom. For many teachers, this represents a significant shift in perspective and behavior. Paying attention to your own and other teachers' concerns is vital.

Reviewing and planning. A simple reviewing and planning process looks at what needs to happen for the plan to work. You may need to review a range of considerations, including staffing, adjusting schedules, developing activities, working with the physical environment, and talking with parents.

Taking action. Some teachers feel comfortable just opening the door and giving it a try with minimal planning. It's important not to get bogged down in planning and not to defer taking action.

Taking small steps and reviewing and planning as you go. As with many elements of the Outdoor Classroom, once you decide to make a change, you can take the initiative, observe and review the results, and plan your next steps as you go. Here's one possible scenario:

Jane and Mario have a classroom of sixteen four-year-olds next to Lily and Sharelle's classroom of fourteen three-year-olds; both rooms are adjacent to a shared play yard. Although the yard is big enough for both groups to use at the same time, the teachers have always scheduled outdoor time so the classes don't mix. Enthused after attending an Outdoor Classroom workshop on Saturday, Jane and Mario come back on Monday and tell Lily and Sharelle that they want to establish indoor-outdoor flow as a primary feature of their full-day program.

Depending on the attitudes of Lily and Sharelle, this may be exciting news or dead on arrival. It doesn't have to be either. Jane and Mario can implement indoor-outdoor flow during their regular outdoor time and see how it works. Lily and Sharelle can observe what happens, ask how it's going, and pose questions for Jane and Mario to consider. Jane and Mario can start by testing out their idea one day per week. With time, experience, conversation, and a little luck, Lily and Sharelle may be willing to give the change a try once a week. By then, Jane and Mario will have had time to work out some of the kinks so the shared experiment has its best chance for success.

This is but one of several ways the two sets of teachers can approach working with each other's interests. Another possibility is that Lily and Sharelle may be interested in the new idea from the start and eager to try it out right away.

Increasing Outdoor Time

Simply increasing outdoor time is perhaps the most obvious first step to take. It provides benefits similar to those of indoor-outdoor flow and raises similar questions and issues. If it's not accompanied by looking at indoor-outdoor flow, a key question might be "How will the children's indoor activities be duplicated outdoors?" This is a critical question, because a key premise of the Outdoor Classroom is "Everything that is done indoors can be done outdoors."

The first phase of implementation is reviewing your initial evaluation to see if it reveals any weaknesses you need to address before

expanding the time children spend outdoors. In particular, you may want to consider the abilities of the staff and program to do these things:

- support children's activities

- move or replicate indoor activities outdoors

- continue to meet outcome goals for children

- coordinate staffing and handle logistics

If you're not adequately addressing these issues already, you may not be ready to increase the amount of time children spend outdoors. Part of deciding if you're ready is assessing/evaluating the capacity of staff to make changes as they go along. Such changes require the following:

- ability to observe and record children's ongoing activities
- sufficient meeting time to discuss and plan changes
- financial resources to pay for changes that require funding

An integral part of expanding children's time outdoors is involving the children themselves. It is, after all, their space, established for their use and benefit. Usually teachers obtain children's input by observing their behavior, but you can also get it directly. For children three and four years of age, talk with them about spending more time outdoors and find out what they most like to do there. Since an objective of the Outdoor Classroom is fostering children's initiative, you might want to hold a brief circle time at the beginning of the day to help children identify their interests.

Relinquishing Teachers' Control—Ensuring Safety

Because of the emphasis on safety first in traditional models of ECE, most teachers have been indoctrinated to believe they must always remain in control. This message is amplified by regulatory agencies, which sometimes behave as if they are enforcing a zero-tolerance rule on children ever becoming injured (for example, in one instance they banished the use of cotton swabs for painting).

While no one wants to see children hurt, keeping children safe is not just a supervisory task requiring controlling behavior by adults; it is just as importantly an educational one. Effective supervision of children needs to be thought of as a teaching task—teaching children to "self-supervise." This is a skill to be learned for life and is a key element of what is required to become a responsible adult. Children learn safety best through direct experience. Teachers must learn to relinquish control so children can have direct experiences and learn for themselves. At the same time, teachers should become engaged in what children are doing so they can help children learn how to take initiative and still stay safe.

Helping children take initiative is at the core of the Outdoor Classroom's philosophy. By definition, this is not a tidy process—true learning is never a tidy process! Supporting children's initiative means supporting their risk taking. It means helping them identify and learn from their mistakes. All of this takes time and patience. It isn't as convenient as a direct "Stop that! It's not safe!" but it is much more instructive.

Supporting Children's Engagement

Engagement is the most important measure of the quality of work that children and teachers do together. Supporting children's engagement means that teachers, too, must be engaged. Such engagement is fairly easy to identify: children stay with activities for long periods; their movements around the play yard are purposeful; they work successfully in groups; they expand their projects to more complex ones. Few behavioral problems occur because children are preoccupied with their activities.

Such scenarios don't happen by accident. Teachers are instrumental in creating environments where children play this way. You need to support children in every way possible for the program and the children to be successful.

Most evaluation instruments do not evaluate teachers' levels of engagement. But you know it when you see it—much like children, engaged teachers reveal a lot through their behavior: they're always active in the yard; they're close to children and their activities; they're present and available without interfering; they frequently interact with children. They show their interest in children and their activities by answering questions, provoke further activity and skill development, provide supplies, and support children's problem solving.

Considering Desired Outcomes

Development of the Outdoor Classroom provides an opportunity to review the developmental outcomes for children that have been previously adopted by the center and determine if they still apply or if the new Outdoor Classroom has created opportunities for additional outcomes that were not previously possible. For instance, if the yard previously had few or no natural elements and the new Outdoor Classroom yard has many more, you may be able to create outcomes for children that involve exposure to and greater understanding and use of items found in nature. You may also find that there are outcomes you should remove from the list because implementing the Outdoor Classroom has changed your center's priorities.

One way to consider a change in outcomes is to think about what children are learning or doing differently than they did before.

Examples of changes in outcome include children doing the following:

- taking more initiative because they are outdoors and have more freedom of movement

- increasing their gross-motor activities, such as climbing, running, and playing group field games

- understanding nature better, such as the names of plants and trees, weather conditions, and natural processes like growing food

- thinking differently about math and science because of being outdoors

If you have not yet developed a set of child outcomes, do so, taking into consideration the changes you observe in the Outdoor Classroom as it currently exists.

Establishing Activity Centers

An essential part of the Outdoor Classroom is its activity centers. The most important point to remember while you're implementing the program is that each activity needs an outdoor home, its own space, just as it does indoors. Some of these spaces may be permanent, like those for swings or a sandbox. Some may move locations, like places for reading books, playing with water, or using loose parts on the grass. Even though these activities may move, the spaces in which they can occur should be identified.

Before implementing the Outdoor Classroom, staff members should compile a list of all the activities they and the children want to take outside and then identify the following:

- how these activities will be accommodated in the yard

- where storage will be located (if indoors, specify how materials will be brought outdoors)

- how activities will be carried out in different weather and seasons

- how children can identify areas to use for specific activities

- how staff will be assigned responsibility for the space

- what kinds of maintenance will be required

Staff need to be certain that activity areas are designated and established, function harmoniously, and do not create problems of access.

Supporting Child-Created Activities

The goal of child-created and child-led activities requires different approaches from you who teach than teacher-directed activities do. Instead of deciding what children should do, you need to observe children's interests and support those. You do this while bearing in mind the program's outcome objectives for children. You facilitate play that helps children reach those outcomes while encouraging them to pursue their own interests as well.

To accomplish these simultaneous tasks, you must be engaged: close enough to the children and their activities to be accurate and effective in the support you offer. Working closely with the children helps you understand their play and the learning that's occurring. You monitor individual progress and make interventions as needed to help children develop their skills and acquire knowledge.

These are keys to effectively supporting children in their own activities:

- **Recognizing and accepting.** The first step in supporting children's activities is recognizing them. This may seem obvious, but to the untrained eye, children's activities may appear to be unfocused and unintentional. Being able to discern what is going on during children's play is a skill acquired through experience. Careful observation and listening are needed to learn what's going on in children's minds.

- **Identifying children's needs.** Skilled teachers observe play and can tell from visual cues and scraps of conversation what children are doing and how their play needs to be supported. Even then you may need to establish a relationship with the children without disrupting their play to be fully effective. Move close enough so the children can engage you in conversation. Closer proximity also gives you the opportunity to comment on their play, make observations, and, if appropriate, ask questions. Beyond such scaffolding, you shouldn't interfere or disrupt their activities.

- **Fostering self-support.** The first focus of support should be to strengthen children's ability to do things themselves. Only after you see that they have exhausted their own ideas should you provide help.

- **Providing material support.** If obtaining supplies is easy because they're close by or readily available, you can suggest to the children that they get them themselves. This helps them learn what's needed to accomplish the tasks they've set for themselves. If their project is at a critical phase, you may want to allow them to keep going while you obtain supplies for them.

- **Providing informational and psychological support.** Activity support includes more than help with supplies. When you're truly engaged, you place yourself in the best position to help children learn and grow through their own activities. Children benefit from a full spectrum of appropriate questions, comments, and cues from you. The trick is to provide them in ways that support their activities rather than disrupting them. Here are some useful forms of contribution:

  Describing what you observe. Simply verbalizing what you see can help children understand more about what they're doing.

  Posing a provocative question. By posing questions like "What do you think would happen if . . . ?" you can help children expand their thinking and problem solve on their own.

  Responding to questions. Children's questions pose opportunities and challenges for you. Their number can be an important indicator of program quality, because questions often mirror the extent of children's engagement in their activities.

As a teacher, you probably find it easier to respond to questions than not. So your specific challenge is to encourage children to try to answer their own questions. You can scaffold this process by providing children with a little bit of information to help them along. You can also encourage them to talk among themselves to find answers. In some circumstances, providing direct and complete answers to a child's query can be the best choice to help him. Here's an example:

(Marcello, age three, is trying to build a tower out of sand by turning a bucket of dry sand upside down.)

M: Teacher, my castle keeps falling down.

T: Why do you think that is?

M: I don't know. I don't know how to keep it up.

T: What kind of sand are you using?

M: This sand, right here. *(He points to the sand in a dry portion of the box.)*

T: Maybe you could try some other sand. Why don't you try the sand over there? *(She points to wet sand in the box. Marcello tries the wet sand and is successful.)*

M: Look, Teacher, I made the castle stand up all by itself!

T: Congratulations, Marcello. I see you were successful. What was different about the new sand?

M: I don't know . . . It was colder. Maybe that's why. It was cold like ice cream!

T: Was there anything else different about it?

M: I don't know. I didn't taste it.

T: Was it dry or wet?

M: It was wet!

T: Why don't you make the dry sand you were playing with earlier wet and see what happens?

M: Will you make it wet with the hose?

T: How about I let you hold the hose while I turn on the water?

M: Oh boy! Sally *(a girl nearby)*—I get to hold the hose!

In this anecdote, the teacher used a variety of responses to encourage Marcello to explore, investigate, analyze, experiment, and develop a conclusion, largely on his own. But she did not leave him totally to his own devices, and when his thinking veered off course, she provided a little scaffolding to help him learn something new. She made it possible for Marcello to have the experience of doing it himself.

A critical part of supporting children's activities is to spend time observing and recording what children see and then to reflect with your fellow staff on these activities. Staff meeting time is essential to properly carry out these discussions. Staff members need enough information and time to coordinate children's activities on a global level. This means looking at the yard, the program, and the staffing as an interactive whole and making sure that all three elements work together harmoniously. When you are working in the Outdoor Classroom, you should be aware of all three elements and how they are functioning. Let's look at an example.

Marci, a newly hired teacher, is pushing one child on the swing and observing a group of approximately twenty children engaged in five different activities on the large, grassy lawn in the center of the play yard. Seven children are busy at the water table, four boys are playing soccer, five children are building with milk crates, and four girls have dragged a blanket right into the middle of the lawn, where one is reading to the other three. The other twenty of the total of forty four-year-olds are scattered around the edges of the yard, as are their four teachers. Felix is over by the sandbox, where seven children are constructing a long ditch. Lisa is at a table overseeing the collage activity of five children. Although the twenty children are playing fairly harmoniously, Marci wonders if she should abandon what she's doing and move into the yard. The little girl she is pushing on the swing has asked to be pushed, and Marci is unsure what to do. She decides to stay where she is, not wanting her young charge to become upset and not wishing to shout across the yard at the other teachers. She plans to ask what she should have done during the staff meeting at the end of the week.

Marci's dilemma demonstrates how easy it is for a new teacher to be uncertain about her role, the roles of others, the use of the yard, and the activities of the children. In the staff meeting, she will ask her colleagues how each determines where to be in the yard and how to evaluate where and when a teacher needs to be present. She will get advice about how to move from being with a single child once she feels she should be with a group. The others will explain the unwritten guidelines about where children can read books on a blanket. Finally, Marci will learn how to communicate effectively with other teachers across the play yard.

Summary

A true Outdoor Classroom offers specific program elements and several qualities unique to each element, including these:

- **Indoor-outdoor flow of children.** When possible, maximize the time that doors are left open so children can move in and out freely.

- **Increased outdoor time for children.** Increase the amount of time children can spend outdoors as close as possible to 50 percent.

- **Relinquishing teachers' control.** Shift control over the activities of children from teachers to the children themselves.

- **Supporting children's initiative.** Encourage children's initiative by making supplies available and encouraging children's independent actions.

- **Being an engaged teacher.** Learn engagement by observing and maintaining appropriate distances from children's activities.

- **Manifesting desired outcomes.** Specify the learning outcomes your program wants children's activities to achieve.

- **Operating specific activity centers.** Specify the space in which each outdoor activity should take place. Spaces should be organized so that different activities can function harmoniously alongside each other.

- **Supporting the creation of specific activities.** So children can learn successfully through their activities, support them by scaffolding and posing provocative questions.

Reflection

On a scale of 1 to 3, with 1 being "employing very fully" and 3 "not employing much at all," rate how well your center applies each of the implementation strategies listed in this chapter. If you rated any strategies as 3 (or 2, if none were rated 3), identify an action you or others in your center can take to use the strategy more frequently.

Outdoor Classroom Staff Perception Survey

Outdoor Classroom Staff Perception Survey

Your Name _____

Name of Center _____

General Instructions

While responding to each question in this survey, **PLEASE THINK ABOUT YOUR EXPERIENCE OVER THE <u>PAST 12 MONTHS.</u>** Please answer ALL the questions; please answer as honestly and completely as you can. Please answer the questions <u>based on your experience only</u>; we want to know what YOU think!

General Marking Instructions

Please <u>carefully</u> follow the marking instructions for each question and <u>mark only in the spaces provided</u>. Thank you!

QUESTIONS ABOUT CHILDREN

1.0 INSTRUCTIONS: For each of the age groups below, please enter <u>YOUR BEST ESTIMATE</u> of the <u>AVERAGE NUMBER OF HOURS PER DAY</u> a child <u>WHO IS ATTENDING ALL DAY</u> spends <u>AT THE PROGRAM</u>. If you can't estimate and don't know, check the box under *I don't know*. If there are no children of one of the ages listed, check the box under *No children that age in our program*.

	Average hours at the program	I don't know	No children that age in our program
1.1 Children under the age of 12 months	_____	☐	☐
1.2 Children older than 12 months but younger than 24 months (2 years)	_____	☐	☐
1.3 Children older than 24 months (2 years) but younger than 36 months (3 years)	_____	☐	☐
1.4 Children older than 36 months (3 years) but younger than 48 months (4 years)	_____	☐	☐
1.5 Children older than 48 months (4 years) but younger than 60 months (5 years)	_____	☐	☐

Continued page 2

2.0 INSTRUCTIONS: For each of the age groups below, please enter <u>YOUR BEST ESTIMATE</u> of the <u>NUMBER OF HOURS PER DAY</u> a child <u>WHO IS ATTENDING ALL DAY</u>, spends <u>OUTDOORS</u>. If you can't estimate and don't know, check the box under *I don't know*. If there are no children of one of the ages listed, check the box under *No children that age in our program*. CONSIDER THE AVERAGE OVER THE ENTIRE YEAR!

		Hours outside	I don't know	No children that age in our program
2.1	**Children under the age of 12 months**	_____	☐	☐
2.2	**Children older than 12 months but younger than 24 months (2 years)**	_____	☐	☐
2.3	**Children older than 24 months (2 years) but younger than 36 months (3 years)**	_____	☐	☐
2.4	**Children older than 36 months (3 years) but younger than 48 months (4 years)**	_____	☐	☐
2.5	**Children older than 48 months (4 years) but younger than 60 months (5 years)**	_____	☐	☐

3.0	**Does your classroom have an "open door" policy that allows children who are old enough to move freely from inside the classroom to outdoors on the playground the majority of the day? (Note: Answer *yes* for infants and toddlers even <u>if you do this</u> only when weather permits and the children are old enough to move on their own.)**	☐ Yes ▷ go to question 5.0 *(Do not answer question 4.1–4.5)* ☐ No ▷ go to question 4.0

2

4.0 INSTRUCTIONS: For the age groups listed below, on average what is your <u>BEST ESTIMATE</u> of <u>HOW MANY TIMES PER DAY</u> the children go outside? If you can't estimate and don't know, check the box under *I don't know*. If there are no children of one of the ages listed, check the box under *No children that age at our center*.

		Times outside per day	I don't know	No children that age at our center
4.1	Children under the age of 12 months	_____	☐	☐
4.2	Children older than 12 months but younger than 24 months (2 years)	_____	☐	☐
4.3	Children older than 24 months (2 years) but younger than 36 months (3 years)	_____	☐	☐
4.4	Children older than 36 months (3 years) but younger than 48 months (4 years)	_____	☐	☐
4.5	Children older than 48 months (4 years) but younger than 60 months (5 years)	_____	☐	☐

NOTE: If you skipped 4.0–4.5, NOW START AGAIN ON THE NEXT PAGE.

Continued page 4

3

5.0 INSTRUCTIONS: ON AVERAGE, OVER THE PERIOD OF A FULL YEAR, when you see children OUTSIDE, <u>HOW FREQUENTLY</u> do you see any children engaged in <u>each</u> of the following activities outside? (Please check a box for each item.)

- If the activity of the question is <u>developmentally INAPPROPRIATE</u> for the age group(s) you usually work with (such as carpentry and infants) <u>please check the box under *Doesn't Apply*</u>.
- HOWEVER, if it IS developmentally appropriate but the program doesn't have the activity, <u>please check the box under *Never*</u>.

	Never	*1-3 times / <u>month</u>*	*1-2 times / <u>week</u>*	*3-4 times / <u>week</u>*	*Daily*	*Doesn't Apply*
5.1 Playing alone	☐	☐	☐	☐	☐	☐
5.2 Playing together with 1–3 other children	☐	☐	☐	☐	☐	☐
5.3 Playing together with 4 or more children	☐	☐	☐	☐	☐	☐
5.4 Group projects (working together to build or develop something)	☐	☐	☐	☐	☐	☐
5.5 Teacher-facilitated circle or group time	☐	☐	☐	☐	☐	☐
5.6 Large (gross) motor activity of any kind	☐	☐	☐	☐	☐	☐
5.7 Running	☐	☐	☐	☐	☐	☐
5.8 Climbing	☐	☐	☐	☐	☐	☐
5.9 Riding or using trikes or other wheel toys	☐	☐	☐	☐	☐	☐
5.10 On swings	☐	☐	☐	☐	☐	☐
5.11 Free-form field games (catch, kicking balls, tossing Frisbees, dancing etc.)	☐	☐	☐	☐	☐	☐
5.12 Organized field games (baseball, basketball, football, soccer, etc.)	☐	☐	☐	☐	☐	☐
5.13 Playing with loose parts/items (hollow blocks, milk crates, cardboard boxes, etc.)	☐	☐	☐	☐	☐	☐
5.14 Small (fine) motor activity of any kind	☐	☐	☐	☐	☐	☐
5.15 Playing with unit blocks or table blocks	☐	☐	☐	☐	☐	☐
5.16 Playing with sand or dirt	☐	☐	☐	☐	☐	☐
5.17 Playing with water	☐	☐	☐	☐	☐	☐
5.18 Gardening /caring for the environment	☐	☐	☐	☐	☐	☐
5.19 Exploring nature (hunting bugs, collecting leaves, watching for birds, etc.)	☐	☐	☐	☐	☐	☐
5.20 Doing table activities of any kind	☐	☐	☐	☐	☐	☐

4

	Never	1–3 times / month	1–2 times / week	3–4 times / week	Daily	Doesn't Apply
5.21 Woodworking and carpentry (hammer, nails, and wood)	☐	☐	☐	☐	☐	☐
5.22 Arts and crafts (activities using a mix of items, such as collage)	☐	☐	☐	☐	☐	☐
5.23 Clay, playdough, sculpturelike activities, etc.	☐	☐	☐	☐	☐	☐
5.24 Reading (looking at books, being read to, reading to self)	☐	☐	☐	☐	☐	☐
5.25 Science-related activities (growing plants, caring for animals, conducting experiments)	☐	☐	☐	☐	☐	☐
5.26 Math-related activities (measuring, counting, games requiring math)	☐	☐	☐	☐	☐	☐
5.27 Doing activities outside that they do inside	☐	☐	☐	☐	☐	☐
5.28 Dramatic play (dress up, playhouse, pretend games)	☐	☐	☐	☐	☐	☐
5.29 Playing musical instruments	☐	☐	☐	☐	☐	☐
5.30 Singing	☐	☐	☐	☐	☐	☐
5.31 Dancing / creative movement	☐	☐	☐	☐	☐	☐
5.32 Painting (all types)	☐	☐	☐	☐	☐	☐
5.33 Lunch and/or snack	☐	☐	☐	☐	☐	☐
5.34 Cleanup	☐	☐	☐	☐	☐	☐

	Never	Sometimes	Often	Frequently	Always	Doesn't Apply
6.0 Overall, when the children play outside, they play happily.	☐	☐	☐	☐	☐	☐
7.0 The equipment and activity areas that are currently available in the playground are being used.	☐	☐	☐	☐	☐	☐
8.0 When playing outside, children are successful in resolving their conflicts with other children with little or no teacher assistance.	☐	☐	☐	☐	☐	☐
9.0 When playing outside, children are effective in starting and completing their own play activities with little or no teacher assistance.	☐	☐	☐	☐	☐	☐

Continued page 6

5

QUESTIONS ABOUT ADULTS

Answer for those adults that you know well enough to comment on.

	Strongly Disagree	Disagree	Somewhat Disagree/Agree	Agree	Strongly Agree	Don't Know
10.0 I'm enthusiastic about getting the children outside.	☐	☐	☐	☐	☐	☐
11.0 My co-teachers are enthusiastic about getting the children outside.	☐	☐	☐	☐	☐	☐
12.0 The teachers in our program agree about the philosophy and practices of our program.	☐	☐	☐	☐	☐	☐
13.0 Our teaching staff are open to change and new ideas concerning our curriculum.	☐	☐	☐	☐	☐	☐
14.0 Our teaching staff have demonstrated success in making program changes.	☐	☐	☐	☐	☐	☐
15.0 Among our teaching staff, there is leadership in place to further develop our outdoor program.	☐	☐	☐	☐	☐	☐
16.0 Among our teaching staff, there is enthusiasm to further develop our outdoor program.	☐	☐	☐	☐	☐	☐
17.0 Our director supports further development of our outdoor program.	☐	☐	☐	☐	☐	☐
18.0 Our director has demonstrated success in achieving program changes.	☐	☐	☐	☐	☐	☐
19.0 Our parents support further development of our outdoor program.	☐	☐	☐	☐	☐	☐
20.0 Our board or owner or administration above our director supports further development of our outdoor program.	☐	☐	☐	☐	☐	☐

6

QUESTIONS ABOUT PROGRAM

Please consider the <u>PROGRAM as a whole</u>, even parts you do not participate in.
(If you don't "know" provide your best "estimate.")

21.0 On average, how many <u>times per month</u> do you attend <u>any</u> type of staff meeting (staff/team/classroom, inservice, program planning, other)?	_____ times
22.0 On average, how many <u>total hours per month</u> do you spend in staff meetings?	_____ hours
23.0 Do the classrooms in your program have at least one door that opens directly out onto the outdoor playground?	☐ Yes ☐ Some do and some don't ☐ No
24.0 Does any portion of the children's playground have to be shared by groups of children who may not play together at the same time because of the difference in their ages (e.g., infants with school-age children)?	☐ Yes ☐ No
25.0 Do the children's playgrounds have enough space for all the children who use that playground to play at the same time?	☐ No ☐ Somewhat ☐ Yes
26.0 Are the children's playgrounds a place of beauty?	☐ No ☐ Somewhat ☐ Yes
27.0 Do the children's playgrounds have enough areas for gardening?	☐ No ☐ Somewhat ☐ Yes
28.0 How often does the center conduct a formal walk-through safety check to make sure the equipment and grounds are safe for children to play on?	☐ Never ☐ 1–6 times/year ☐ Weekly ☐ Daily ☐ Monthly ☐ Don't Know

	Strongly Disagree	Disagree	Somewhat Disagree/Agree	Agree	Strongly Agree	Don't Know
29.0 Teaching staff are likely to conduct an activity outside that is usually done inside.	☐	☐	☐	☐	☐	☐
30.0 When outdoors, teaching staff are actively involved in supervising children's play.	☐	☐	☐	☐	☐	☐
31.0 When outdoors, teaching staff are actively involved in interacting with the children.	☐	☐	☐	☐	☐	☐
32.0 There are adequate quantities and kinds of toys and activity materials for outdoor play.	☐	☐	☐	☐	☐	☐

Continued page 8

	Not at all	Somewhat	Mostly	Enough	Too much/ many
33.0 Do the children's playgrounds have enough space for children to run freely and play running games?	☐	☐	☐	☐	☐
34.0 Do the children's playgrounds have enough space for all types of activities and program elements that children need to have outdoors (such as climbing structures, shade, trike paths, grass, sand, water)?	☐	☐	☐	☐	☐
35.0 Do the children's playgrounds have enough shade?	☐	☐	☐	☐	☐
36.0 Do the children's playgrounds have enough sun?	☐	☐	☐	☐	☐
37.0 Do the children's playgrounds have enough grass?	☐	☐	☐	☐	☐
38.0 Do the children's playgrounds have enough hard surface (for wheel toys, ball games)?	☐	☐	☐	☐	☐
39.0 Do the children's playgrounds have enough trees?	☐	☐	☐	☐	☐
40.0 Do the children's playgrounds have enough plants?	☐	☐	☐	☐	☐
41.0 Do the children's playgrounds have enough space for sand and water play?	☐	☐	☐	☐	☐
42.0 Do the children's playgrounds have enough natural area where children can explore nature?	☐	☐	☐	☐	☐
43.0 Do the children's playgrounds have enough space for trikes and wheel toys?	☐	☐	☐	☐	☐
44.0 Do the children's playgrounds have enough equipment?	☐	☐	☐	☐	☐
45.0 Do the children's playgrounds have enough storage?	☐	☐	☐	☐	☐
46.0 Do the children's playgrounds have sufficient visibility to allow for adequate supervision?	☐	☐	☐	☐	☐

8

The Outdoor Classroom Project

ONCE A CENTER has embarked on the task of developing their Outdoor Classroom, the greatest challenge is to continue. Recognizing this, the Outdoor Classroom Project provides continuing support in the form of ongoing training through workshops and conferences, play yard consultations and design, and opportunities to participate in networks of sites that have achieved "Recognized" or "Demonstration" Outdoor Classroom site status.

What Is the Outdoor Classroom Project?

The Outdoor Classroom Project is the vehicle by which the practice of the Outdoor Classroom is formally articulated and presented. The Project was initially funded in July of 2003 through a five-year, $1 million grant from First 5 LA, which disperses funds generated by California's Proposition 10 tobacco tax to projects serving children ages zero to five years in Los Angeles County. Now focused in Santa Barbara County, where it has reached over 80 percent of the 180 licensed centers with funding from the Orfalea Foundations, the project has reached over 2,000 centers and over 6,000 teachers throughout California and nationally where it regularly collaborates with Nature Explore. The Project is an initiative of the Child Educational Center, Caltech/JPL Community (CEC), a nationally accredited program of early childhood education. More may be found at the Outdoor Classroom website www .outdoorclassroomproject.org.

About the Child Educational Center

The Child Educational Center (CEC) is the model site for the Outdoor Classroom Project. Outdoor Classroom philosophy, principles, and practices were developed over a period of nearly twenty-five years of working with hundreds of children, ages two months through five years of age, at its preschool site in La Canada, California. It continues its ongoing evolution of the Outdoor Classroom every day.

The CEC is a nonprofit educational organization providing developmental, research-based care and education for more than seven hundred children through a model program delivered by 130 staff at seven sites. It was established in 1979 at the request of the Jet Propulsion Laboratory, a NASA-funded research center operated by the California Institute of Technology. Through its $7 million annual budget, the CEC serves children ages six weeks through twelve years of age with a variety of age-appropriate care and education. Its infant-toddler/preschool program has been continuously accredited by the National Association for the Education of Young Children (NAEYC) since 1988. Envisioned and designed from its beginning as a learning community, the CEC has evolved into a unique organization, rich with innovative and practical educational models. These models are utilized by ECE professionals, college students, clients of the CEC's consulting and training division, Child Care Planning Associates, and most recently, participants in the CEC's Outdoor Classroom Project. More may be found at the CEC website: www.ceconline.org.

Outdoor Classroom Project Activities

Following are descriptions of the Outdoor Classroom Project's activities and services:

- funded initiatives
- training and staff development, including specialist training
- center site consultation
- outdoor classroom demonstration and recognized sites and networks
- research

In addition to the project descriptions below, more details and a current calendar can be obtained from the Outdoor Classroom Project website: http://outdoorclassroomproject.org/.

Funded Initiatives

The largest of the Project's activities have been its funded multiyear initiatives in Los Angeles and Santa Barbara Counties in California. These initiatives implement training and play yard upgrades to transform the way in which the outdoors is used in a region's programs of early care and education. Funded initiatives are generally multiyear endeavors and paid for by the funder. All other services provided by the Project that are not funded initiatives are provided for a fee.

Training and Staff Development, Including Specialist Training

The Project delivers a wide variety of subject matter through conferences and single workshops that are held both at the CEC model site and locations of clients' choosing, including individual center sites. The *Outdoor Classroom Specialist Series* is provided similarly. The specialist series currently comprises three modules, each of which is held on one Saturday a month over a three-to-four-month period. Participants earn a certificate of completion for each module fully attended.

Center Site Consultation

Evaluation and recommendations on outdoor program operation and yard design are available to individual centers. Yard design evaluations can also be done remotely without a physical site visit.

Outdoor Classroom Demonstration and Recognized Sites and Networks

Part of the mission of the Outdoor Classroom Project is to support the permanent existence of a substantial number of early childhood centers with high-quality Outdoor Classrooms as a fundamental part of the center program. Centers that have initially participated with the Outdoor Classroom Project via consulting or training can continue their involvement through participation as a recognized site or demonstration site. These programs have achieved, or are in the process of achieving, a certain level of proficiency in Outdoor Classroom philosophy, principles, and practices.

Such sites are organized into Outdoor Classroom networks according to geographic region. The Outdoor Classroom Project operates the Recognized and Demonstration site application process and oversees the cultivation, creation, and operation of the networks. Additional information can be found on the Outdoor Classroom website.

Research

The Project participates in ongoing national research on the value of outdoor play for children, including a multiyear research project with the Dimensions Educational Research Foundation.

Resources for Early Childhood Educators

Books

Banning, Wendy, and Ginny Sullivan. 2010. *Lens on Outdoor Learning*. St. Paul, MN: Redleaf Press.

Carter, Margie, and Deb Curtis. 1998. *The Visionary Director: A Handbook for Dreaming, Organizing, and Improvising in Your Center*. St. Paul, MN: Redleaf Press.

———. 2003. *Designs for Living and Learning: Transforming Early Childhood Environments*. St. Paul, MN: Redleaf Press.

Chalufour, Ingrid, and Karen Worth. 2003. *Discovering Nature with Young Children*. St. Paul, MN: Redleaf Press.

Child Care Planning Associates. 2010. *Child Care Design and Siting Guidelines*. Pasadena, CA: First 5 Riverside.

Cornell, Joseph. 1998. *Sharing Nature with Children*. Nevada City, CA: Dawn Publications.

———. 1999. *Sharing Nature with Children II*. Nevada City, CA: Dawn Publications.

Crain, William. 2003. *Reclaiming Childhood*. New York: Henry Holt and Co.

Cross, Aerial. 2011. *Nature Sparks: Connecting Children's Learning to the Natural World*. St. Paul, MN: Redleaf Press.

Danks, Fiona. 2006. *Nature's Playground*. London: Frances Lincoln.

Dannenmaier, Molly. 1998. *A Child's Garden: Enchanting Outdoor Spaces for Children and Parents*. New York: Simon & Schuster.

DeBord, Karen, Linda Hestenes, Robin Moore, Nilda Cosco, and Janet McGinnis. 2005. *POEMS: Preschool Outdoor Environment Measurement Scale (POEMS)*. Lewisville, NC: Kaplan Early Learning Company.

Elkind, David. 2007. *The Power of Play*. Cambridge, MA: Da Capo Lifelong Books.

Eriksen, Aase. 1985. *Playground Design: Outdoor Environments for Learning and Development.* New York: Van Nostrand Reinhold.

Greenman, Jim. 1988. *Caring Spaces, Learning Places: Children's Environments That Work.* Redmond, WA: Exchange Press.

———. 1998. *Places for Childhoods: Making Quality Happen in the Real World.* Redmond, WA: Exchange Press.

Clifford, Richard, Debby Cryer, and Thelma Harms. 1998. *Early Childhood Environment Rating Scale.* New York: Teachers College Press.

Helm, Judy Harris, and Sallee Beneke. 2003. *The Power of Projects.* New York: Teachers College Press.

Helm, Judy Harris, and Lillian Katz. 2000. *Young Investigators: The Project Approach in the Early Years.* New York: Teachers College Press.

Jones, Elizabeth. 1994. *Emergent Curriculum.* Washington, DC: NAEYC.

Jones, Elizabeth, and Renatta M. Cooper. 2005. *Playing to Get Smart.* New York: Teachers College Press.

Jones, Elizabeth, and Gretchen Reynolds. 1992. *The Play's the Thing.* New York: Teachers College Press.

Keeler, Rusty. 2008. *Natural Playscapes.* Redmond, WA: Exchange Press.

Koralek, Derry, and Laura J. Colker, eds. 2003. *Spotlight on Young Children and Science.* Washington, DC: NAEYC.

Kutska Kenneth, Kevin Hoffman, and Antonio Malkusak. 2002. *Playground Safety Is No Accident.* NRPA/NPSI/PDRMA.

Louv, Richard. 2005. *Last Child in the Woods: Saving Children from Nature-Deficit Disorder.* Chapel Hill, NC: Algonquin Books.

———. *The Nature Principle: Human Restoration and the End of Nature-Deficit Disorder.* Chapel Hill, NC: Algonquin Books.

Medved, Michael, and Diane Medved. 1998. *Saving Childhood, Protecting Our Children from the National Assault on Innocence.* New York: Harper Perennial.

Mooney, Carol Garhart. 2000. *Theories of Childhood: An Introduction to Dewey, Montessori, Erikson, Piaget & Vygotsky.* St. Paul, MN: Redleaf Press.

Moore, Robin, and Herbert Wong. 1997. *Natural Learning: Creating Environments for Rediscovering Nature's Way of Teaching.* Berkeley, CA: Mig Communications.

Moore, Robin, Susan Goltsman, and Daniele Iacofano, eds. 1992. *Play for All Guidelines: Planning, Design, and Management of Outdoor Play Settings for All Children,* 2nd ed. Berkeley, CA: Mig Communications.

Nabhan, Gary Paul, and Stephen Trimble. 1994. *The Geography of Childhood: Why Children Need Wild Places.* Boston, MA: Beacon Press.

Nature Explore. 2007. *Learning with Nature Idea Book: Creating Nurturing Outdoor Spaces for Children.* Lincoln, NE: Arbor Day Foundation.

Nature Explore. 2011 *Growing with Nature Book: Supporting Whole-Child Learning in Outdoor Classrooms.* Lincoln, NE: Dimensions Educational Research Foundation.

Olds, Anita Rui. 2000. *Child Care Design Guide.* New York: McGraw-Hill.

Palmer, Parker. 1998. *The Courage to Teach.* San Francisco: Jossey-Bass.

Rivkin, Mary S. 1995. *The Great Outdoors.* Washington, DC: National Association for the Education of Young Children.

Roca, Nuria. 2007. *The Three R's: Reuse, Reduce, Recycle.* Barron's Educational Series.

Shore, Rima. 1997. *Rethinking the Brain: New Insights into Early Development.* New York: Families and Work Institute.

Shuttlesworth, Dorothy Edwards. 2010. *Exploring Nature with Your Child: An Introduction to the Enjoyment and Understanding of Nature.* Charleston, SC: Nabu Press.

Sobel, David, and Robert Ornstein. 1996. *The Healthy Mind, Healthy Body Handbook.* New York: Patient Education Media, Inc.

Sobel, D. 1996. *Beyond Ecophobia: Reclaiming the Heart in Nature Education.* Great Barrington, MA: The Orion Society.

Stine, Sharon. 1997. *Landscapes for Learning: Creating Outdoor Environments for Children and Youth.* New York: John Wiley & Sons.

Ward, Jennifer. 2008. *I Love Dirt.* Boston, MA: Trumpeter Books.

Worth, Karen, and Sharon Grollman. 2003. *Worms, Shadows, and Whirlpools: Science in the Early Childhood Classroom.* Washington, DC: NAEYC.

Video

Great Places for Childhood: Children's Environments That Work, produced by Bright Horizons, the Enterprise Foundation, Kaplan.

New Dimensions to Learning, produced by Nature Explore.

Learning with Nature, produced by Nature Explore.

Reading Opportunities for Children

Allen, Judy. 2000. *Are You a Butterfly?* Boston, MA: Kingfisher.

Aston, Dianna. 2006. *An Egg Is Quiet.* San Francisco: Chronicle Books.

Castella, Krystina, and Brian Boyl. 2005. *Discovering Nature's Alphabet.* Berkeley, CA: Heyday Books.

Craighead, Charles. 1994. *The Eagle and the River.* New York: Macmillan.

Mannis, Celeste Davidson. 2006. *Snapshots: The Wonders of Monterey Bay.* New York: Viking.

Stanley, Elizabeth. 2007. *Tyger! Tyger!* New York: Enchanted Lion Books.

Strickland, Betsy. 2004. *Low Country A to Z.* Hilton Head Island, SC: Makai Concepts.

Trumbauer, Lisa. 2002. *The Life Cycle of a Butterfly.* Mankato, MN: Capstone Press.

Yard Design Errors

Look at the yard shown in the photograph to the left before reading the list below and see how many design flaws you would identify. Analyzing and discussing yard spaces can enhance your understanding of how complex creating an optimum Outdoor Classroom really is. Most yards are inadequately designed not because of unskilled designers but because there is too little informed input from early childhood educators and a failure to see the space as a learning environment. Discussing the items listed as flaws below with other staff members can facilitate your evaluation of your own center's play yard.

1. No trees to provide shade (this is a hot climate).

2. No shrubs or greenery at child level.

3. No garden area when space is available for garden area.

4. No swings.

5. Shade structure only provides shade at high noon; shade is insufficient to shade sand area most of the day (trees are generally more effective at providing shade).

6. Location of trike paths interferes with children's access to other activity areas.

7. Number of trike pathways are excessive and unnecessary, reducing the available amount of grass.

8. Concrete pathways run in a variety of directions, but don't facilitate meaningful, directional flow of foot traffic to well-defined activity areas.

9. Excessive use of concrete pathways unnecessarily divides the yard.

10. Concrete pathways are wider than necessary, reducing the available amount of grass and incurring unnecessary cost.

11. Extra-wide trike pathways foster two-way trike traffic, which is less safe than one-way traffic.

12. Shared use of concrete paths by trikes and pedestrians creates an inherent traffic conflict.

13. Pattern of concrete pathways creates a chaotic traffic flow for trikes.

14. Overall, trike traffic is inadequately controlled; the trike paths lead directly into the overhung patio next to the building; this is traditionally where tables are placed for outdoor table activities, thus trike traffic and table activities are inappropriately mixed.

15. Small grassy areas in foreground are too little to serve any meaningful activity purpose.

16. Type of grass used (fescue) is too fragile for heavy preschool use; it is not self-repairing, so damaged areas will turn to barren dirt.

17. There is no area in which children can safely run. The "large" space in the middle is too small; the narrow strip of grass at the back is not wide enough, irregular in width, inadequate for field games, such as soccer, and bordered by a curb off of which children could easily fall, if running.

18. The fall height from the top of concrete tunnel could require fall material—grass does not qualify.

19. The activity purpose of the middle grass area is unfocused; the structure in front of the concrete tunnel has no relationship to anything else in the yard.

20. The entire portion of the yard shown (about 2,000 square feet) has no clearly defined, nor protected area of activity focus; it would be difficult for children to develop and sustain an activity for the 45 minutes generally recommended because of constant traffic flow and distraction, lack of visual definition of space with low barriers and shade, and lack of storage.

21. While there is some extra wood fiber fall zone space next to where the slide ends (left side of picture), it isn't big enough for an activity such as building with loose parts like milk crates or tires; thus, it is either too big and wasteful, or too little and not useful.

22. The pillars in the foreground are hazardous in two regards: (1) They have sharp edges, and (2) Above the brick they are faced with sprayed concrete (shotcrete or gunite), which is so rough and abrasive that if a child brushes against, it will tear their skin. This should never be used to surface a child care center where children could brush against it.

23. No outdoor storage is available close to areas where items such as toys and trikes might be used.

Sample of Ideal Scene

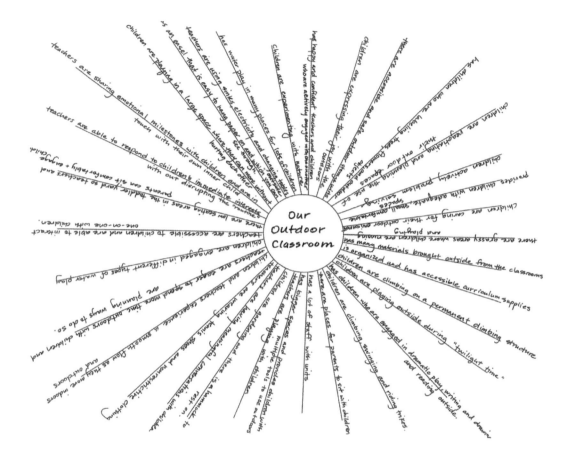

Note: This ideal scene description was developed by teachers in a brainstorming session and shows some types of ideas that might be provided. Because the time span encompassed by an ideal scene can cover years, elements of the ideal scene may not be implemented (as needs change) or may be implemented differently from their original description.

Our Outdoor Classroom . . .

teachers are able to respond to children's immediate interests without disrupting the "routine"

teachers are sharing emotional milestones with children and are in touch with their own inner child

children are playing in a large space where they can move without hurting
each other

has an easel that is easy to hang paper on and which you can see through

teachers are using sinks, electricity and changing tables outside

has water play in many places for lots of children

children are experimenting with nature

has happy and confident teachers and children who are actively engaged
with one another

children are expressing their joy with the outdoors

there are accessible and safe outdoor storage units

has children who are labeling trees, flowers and outdoor objects

children are negotiating and planning the use of their outdoor spaces

children actively problem solving

provides children with adequate, small comfortable spaces

children are caring for their outdoor environment

there are grassy areas where children are running and playing

has many materials brought outside from the classroom

is organized and has accessible curriculum supplies

children are climbing on a permanent climbing structure

children are playing outside during "twilight time"

has children who are engaged in dramatic play, writing and drawing, and
reading outside

children are climbing, swinging and riding trikes

there are places for parents to sit with children

has a lot of staff with [educational] units

has bigger spaces and provides children with multiple tools to use outdoors

teachers are playing with children

children are gardening and there is a hammock to lie in

teachers are having meaningful conversations with children

teachers are wearing tennis shoes and non-restrictive clothing

children and teachers experience a smooth flow as they move indoors and
outdoors

teachers are eager to spend more time outdoors with children and are
planning ways to do so

children are engaged in different types of water play

teachers are accessible to children and are able to interact one-on-one
with children

there are low seating areas in the toddler yard so teachers and parents
can sit comfortably and engage children

References

American Academy of Pediatrics (AAP). 2007. "Early TV Viewing Habits Could Have Lasting Effect on Kids' Attention." www2.aap.org/advocacy/releases /sept07studies.htm.

Larson, Michael F. 2011. "Amphetamine-Related Psychiatric Disorders." Last updated October 27. http://emedicine.medscape.com/ article/289973-overview.

McElroy, Molly. 2011. "40 Percent of Youths Attempting Suicide Make First Attempt before High School." *UW Today*. University of Washington. http://www.washington.edu/news/articles/40-percent-of-youths -attempting-suicide-make-first-attempt-before-high-school.

Medco Health Solutions. 2004. "Medco Study Reveals Pediatric Spending Spike on Drugs to Treat Behavioral Problems." http://phx.corporate-ir.net /phoenix.zhtml?c=131268&p=irol-newsArticle_print&ID=571791&highlight=.

St. Luke's Health Initiatives. 2006. "Trends and Markers." Arizona Health Futures. August: 10–15. www.slhi.org/publications/issue_briefs/pdfs /ib-2006-August.pdf.

Tovey, Helen. 2007. *Playing Outdoors: Spaces and Places, Risk and Challenge*. London: Open University Press.

Index

initial changes (Step 3), 110–113

monitoring, tracking, and evaluating
(Step 6), 121

outcomes, defining (Step 2), 108–109, 157–158

priorities, setting (Step 2), 107–108

questions to ask, 101

developmentally appropriate activities, 12

directors. *See* administrators

drugs. *See* medications

DVD players in cars, 20–21

E

early childhood education (ECE)

curriculum considerations, 11

guiding vision, 7

holistic approach, 11, 33

philosophy of, 1

reductive approaches, 26, 33

Early Childhood Environmental Rating Scale
(ECERS), 126

ECE. *See* early childhood education (ECE)

ECERS. *See* Early Childhood Environmental Rating
Scale (ECERS)

Einstein, Albert, 122

electronic media, use of, 20–22, 29

Elkind, David, 5

emergent curriculums, 55

emotional distress. *See* psychological well-being

employees. *See* staff

engagement

lack of with nature, 25–26

of children, encouraging, 12, 29, 32, 45–46,
156–157

of teachers, 12, 44, 45, 157

enthusiasm, need for, 98

environment

activity centers, 53–54, 159–160

aesthetics of, 137, 143, 144

enriching, 41–42

evaluating, 133–148

hazards, 30, 59, 61, 63

importance of for learning, 8, 10, 46

maintenance issues, 65–67, 90

plants and trees, 61–63

stewardship of, teaching children about, 31

teacher knowledge about, 42

weather and climate, 40–41, 60–61, 113

See also nature; site design

equipment. *See* climbing structures; materials

evaluation

defined, 125

of existing practices, 103

of outdoor space

composition and content, 146–148

form and spatial relationships, 144–145

layout and interfaces, 138–140

purposes of, 133–135

safety, 135–136

size, 141–143

of program implementation, 121

of programs

activities, 130–133

bias in, 126

data gathering process, 126

evaluation tools, 126–130

reasons for, 125

of staff perceptions and attitudes, 127–130,
171–178

of staff readiness for change, 75–77

exercise. *See* physical activity

F

facilitators, teachers as, 50–52

fears

for child safety, 23

impact on early childhood education, 26

of nature, 23–24

financial considerations, 70, 91, 95, 155, 181

reflection exercises

    about stakeholder groups, 89

    childhood experiences, 13

    implementation strategies, 169

    need for professional development, 89

    programs and practices, evaluation of, 14, 35, 67

    readiness for change, 123

relationship-based curriculums, 82

repairs and maintenance, 65–67, 90

resources, 103, 183–185

responsibility

    assigning to team members, 116–117

    for personal development, 81

risks

    environmental hazards, 30, 59, 61, 63

    learning opportunities and, 23, 49–50, 135–136, 155–156

    overprotection of children, 16–18, 23, 43–44, 49–50, 136

rose bushes, 61

S

safety

    child learning about, 23, 49–50, 135–136, 155–156

    media-driven fears about, 23–24

    of outdoor spaces, 30, 135–136, 155–156

    overprotection of children, 16–18, 23, 43–44, 49–50, 136

scaffolding and support, 161–168

schedules. *See* timelines

school readiness

    emphasis on, 56, 79

    facilitating, 33

science skills, 4, 6, 158

shade, providing, 60, 146

short-term strategies for facilitating change, 94

silver maple trees, 61

site design

    activity centers, 53–54, 159–160

    aesthetics, 137, 143, 144

    composition and content, 146–148

    evaluation of, 133–148

    form and spatial relationships, 144–145

    layout and interfaces, 64, 138–140

    maintenance issues, 65–67

    mistakes in, 73, 74, 119, 124, 135, 145

    natural features and plants, 61–63

    safety, 30, 135–136, 155–156

    sample plans, 28, 47, 95

    size of outdoor space, 141–143

    stakeholders in, 69–74

    storage spaces, 52, 64, 113, 132

    teacher knowledge of, need for, 37, 58, 64, 65, 72–73

    weather and climate considerations, 40–41, 60–61

    See also environment; safety

size of outdoor spaces, 141–143

social skills, facilitating, 33

society, as stakeholder, 74

soils, 63

staff

    acknowledging efforts of, 122–123

    attitudes about change, 70, 75–77, 91

    communication skills, 82

    condition of, 76–77

    consensus, obtaining, 108

    group discussions, 103–104

    including in planning, 118

    involvement and implementation, examples of, 83–88

    job satisfaction, 75–77

    Outdoor Classroom Staff Perception Survey, 127–130, 171–178

    professional development, 77–81, 103, 181

    psychologically safe working environments, 78–81

    See also teachers

Image and Photography Credits

Photograph on page iv copyright Edmund Barr, reprinted by permission

Photographs and images on pages xvi, 2, 6, 7, 8, 9 (top right and bottom left), 10 (top left, top right, and bottom left), 12, 14, 16, 25, 29 (left), 32, 33, 34, 36, 38, 40, 41 (top right), 42, 43, 44, 47 (bottom), 49 (center), 52 (right), 53, 56, 57, 60, 62 (top left and bottom), 65 (right), 67, 68, 70, 71, 76, 82, 93, 97, 98, 99, 101, 109, 113, 120, 133, 147, 152, 155, 156, 157, 158, 159, 161, 162, 165, 167 copyright CEC, reprinted by permission

Photograph on page 12 (top) courtesy of Deborah Fath

Photograph on page 19 copyright iStockphoto.com/fatihhoca

Photograph on page 21 copyright iStockphoto.com/LUGO

Photographs on pages 39 and 41 (top left) courtesy of Maria Douvia

Photographs on pages 52 (left), 163, and 164 courtesy of Angélique Whitcomb

Photograph on page 64 (top) by Phil Schermeister, reprinted by permission of PR&P Architects

Photograph on page 84 (bottom) courtesy of Randee Norwood

Image on page 95 courtesy of Michelle FitzGerald Design

The remaining photographs are courtesy of the author

ERIC NELSON co-founded the Child Educational Center, Caltech/JPL Community near Pasadena, CA, in 1979. He is the center's director of consulting and educational services and manages the Outdoor Classroom Project. An adjunct professor since 1977, Eric developed a course on outdoor classrooms, which evolved into a series of outdoor classroom specialist trainings. He presents on a broad range of topics related to outdoor classrooms and consults on play yard design. Eric's understanding of the value of the outdoors is grounded in a lifetime of hiking his beloved Sierra Nevada Mountains in California since he was a young child.